South East Scotland
Edited by Claire Tupholme

First published in Great Britain in 2007 by:
Young Writers
Remus House
Coltsfoot Drive
Peterborough
PE2 9JX
Telephone: 01733 890066
Website: www.youngwriters.co.uk

All Rights Reserved

© Copyright Contributors 2007

SB ISBN 978-1 84431 142 2

Foreword

Young Writers was established in 1991 and has been passionately devoted to the promotion of reading and writing in children and young adults ever since. The quest continues today. Young Writers remains as committed to the nurturing of poetic and literary talent as ever.

This year's Young Writers competition has proven as vibrant and dynamic as ever and we are delighted to present a showcase of the best poetry from across the UK and in some cases overseas. Each poem has been selected from a wealth of *Little Laureates* entries before ultimately being published in this, our sixteenth primary school poetry series.

Once again, we have been supremely impressed by the overall quality of the entries we have received. The imagination, energy and creativity which has gone into each young writer's entry made choosing the poems a challenging and often difficult but ultimately hugely rewarding task - the general high standard of the work submitted ensured this opportunity to bring their poetry to a larger appreciative audience.

We sincerely hope you are pleased with this final collection and that you will enjoy *Little Laureates South East Scotland* for many years to come.

Contents

Clepington Primary School, Dundee

Connor Hunter (8)	1
Shannon Millar (8)	2
Laura Milton (8)	3
Harley Martin (8)	4
Tony Williamson (8)	5
Rebecca McColl (8)	6
Amy Gallacher (8)	7
Robbie Norrie (11)	8
Lewis MacLaughlan (11)	9
Dean Imlay (11)	10
Sarah Green (11)	11
Reece McArtney (11)	12
Aled Bartley-Jones (11)	13
John Joe Fitzpatrick (10)	14
Henna Saleem (10)	15
James Glover (10)	16
Aarron Lee Donaldson (11)	17
Rachel Tonelli (10)	18
Lauren McIntosh (10)	19
Kirsty Jane Gallacher (10)	20
Rachael Strachan (10)	21
Rhys Mackenzie (10)	22
Eilidh Richardson (10)	23
Ali Mahmood (10)	24
Cameron Healy (10)	25
Kayleigh Brough (10)	26
Kieran Sturrock (10)	27
Morgan Ann Low (11)	28
Billy West (10)	29
Abbie Taylor (11)	30
Hannah Scott	31
Astrid Vaughan (10)	32
Jessica Ross (10)	33
Chloe Teale (10)	34
Jared Duncan (10)	35
Callum Wood (10)	36
Lee Kerr (10)	37
David West (10)	38

Lee Collins (10)	39
John Shields (10)	40
Iain Cunningham (11)	41
Rafiq Shakeel (11)	42
Aadam Un-Nabi (10)	43
Zahira Yasin (10)	44
Sinead McDonagh (10)	45
Lucy Hendry (10)	46
Aisha Mahmood (11)	47
Darren Pake (11)	48
Megan Lorimer (11)	49
Kerri Corstorphine (11)	50
Chloe Davidson (11)	51
Lewis Chalmers (11)	52
Heather Heenan (11)	53
Josh Anderson (11)	54
Kieran Philp (11)	55
Anisah Ahmed (11)	56
Iona Boath (11)	57
Zoe Blackwood	58

Crombie Primary School, Crombie

Katie Strachan (9)	59
Isla McLeod (10)	60
Cameron Montgomery (9)	61
Kayleigh Hood (9)	62
AJ Burns (9)	63
Liam Campbell (11)	64
Kyle Smith (11)	65
Holly Roxburgh (9)	66
Toni Marshall (9)	67
Kate Schafferius (10)	68

Inverkeithing Primary School, Inverkeithing

Paige Gardner (11)	69
Francesca McShane (11)	70
Wayne Bridges (11)	71
Melissa Black (11)	72
Shaun Smith (11)	73
Abby Drummond (11)	74
Gemma Park (11)	75

Kourtney Lyness (10)	76
Sarah Clouston (10)	77
Toni-Leigh Watson (10)	78
Alexander Sinclair (11)	79
John Mitchell (10)	80
Christopher Ostrom (10)	81
Lorna Forker (10)	82
Dylan Hall (10)	83
Kayleigh Fosker (10)	84
Emilly Campbell (10)	85
Claire Fairbairn (10)	86
Stuart Milne (10)	87
Daniel Sinclair (10)	88
Kieran Gear (10)	89
Colin Law (10)	90
Christopher Naughton (10)	91

Lynburn Primary School, Dunfermline

Kiera Pick (9)	92
Jamie-Lee Curran (9)	93
Sean Birrell (9)	94
Jacob Stephenson (9)	95
Kayleigh Anne Lindsell (9)	96
Billy-John Jack (9)	97
Sean David Wilson (9)	98
Peter McKean (10)	99
Kerri-Jade Todd (9)	100
Carly Westwater & Chloe Foster (9)	101
Danielle Lafferty (9)	102
Fraser Wilson & Ryan Colbert (9)	103
Sean Carroll (9)	104

St John the Baptist Primary School, Fauldhouse

Rachel Timmins (9)	105
Colette Rowell (9)	106
Jordan McCormick (9)	107
Munro McKay (9)	108
Megan McKenzie (9)	109
Paul Lynch (9)	110
Jake Denholme (9)	111
Meghan Cairns (9)	112

Thomas Warrington (10)	113
Taylor Lamont (9)	114
Bryss Aitchison (9)	115
Jamie Walker (9)	116
Michael Cairney (9)	117
Lesleyanne Nimmo (9)	118
Taylor John Ball (9)	119
Caitlin Hilson (9)	120
Amy Ramsay (9)	121
Kayleigh Reid (9)	122
Teri Flannigan (9)	123
Sophie Halpin (11)	124
Sean McAnna (11)	125
Amy Hunter (11)	126
Steven O'Mullan (12)	127
Demi Malloy (11)	128
Dylan Watson (11)	129
James Mateer (11)	130
Connor Morton	131
Aaron Jack (11)	132
Chloe Findlay (11)	133
Sean Timmins (12)	134
Andrew Hutchison (11)	135
Erin Muirhead (11)	136
David Dalziel (11)	137
Robyn Ovens (11)	138
Iqra Ramzan (9)	139
Maree Rooney (10)	140
Johnnie Sommerville (9)	141
Cameron Bennett (9)	142

St Peter's Primary School, Edinburgh

Michelangelo Mario Antonio Mulholland (10)	143
Kieran Watt (10)	144
Glen Paterson (9)	145
Josh Proctor (9)	146
Nathan Speedman (9)	147
Christopher Turnbull (10)	148
Theresa Wong (9)	149
Anna Service (10)	150
Sally Cairns (10)	151

Jacob Kennedy (10)	152
James Flynn (10)	153
Michael Monan 10)	154
Molly Donovan (10)	155
Peter Rennie (10)	156
Emily McHugh (10)	157
Charlotte McGowan (10)	158
Kieran Fitzgerald (10)	159
Daniel Pacitti (10)	160
Gilian Reid (10)	161
Tom Jarvis (10)	162
Rian McDermott (10)	163
Daniella McGinley (9)	164
Ellen McGrath (9)	165
Matthew Messer (9)	166
Patrick Mulvanny (9)	167
Kirsty Anderson (9)	168
Jack Crookston (10)	169
John Dunn-Butler (9)	170
Louise Goode (9)	171
Amanda Kostryckyj (9)	172
Gianluca Cuthbertson (9)	173

Wardle Primary School, Edinburgh

Kirsty Summers (9)	174
Hayley Scott (9)	175
Aaron Heinemeier (9)	176
Louis Malcolm (9)	177
Freya Dixon-van Dijk (9)	178
Nancy Brown (9)	179
Matthew Fischbacher (9)	180
Marcus Chapman (9)	181

Wormit Primary School, Wormit

Cameron Soutar (9)	182
John Nelson (10)	183
Megan Dempster (10)	184
Alexander Rowan (9)	185
Rebecca Weir (9)	186
Susannah Rosemary McWhirter (9)	187
Freya Simpson (9)	188

Eve Gourlay (9)	189
Clodagh Ryan (9)	190
Robin Black (10)	191
Adam Nish (9)	192
Anne-Marie Marshall (9)	193
Eleanor Heighton (9)	194
Phoebe Martin (9)	195
Rory Strathie (9)	196

The Poems

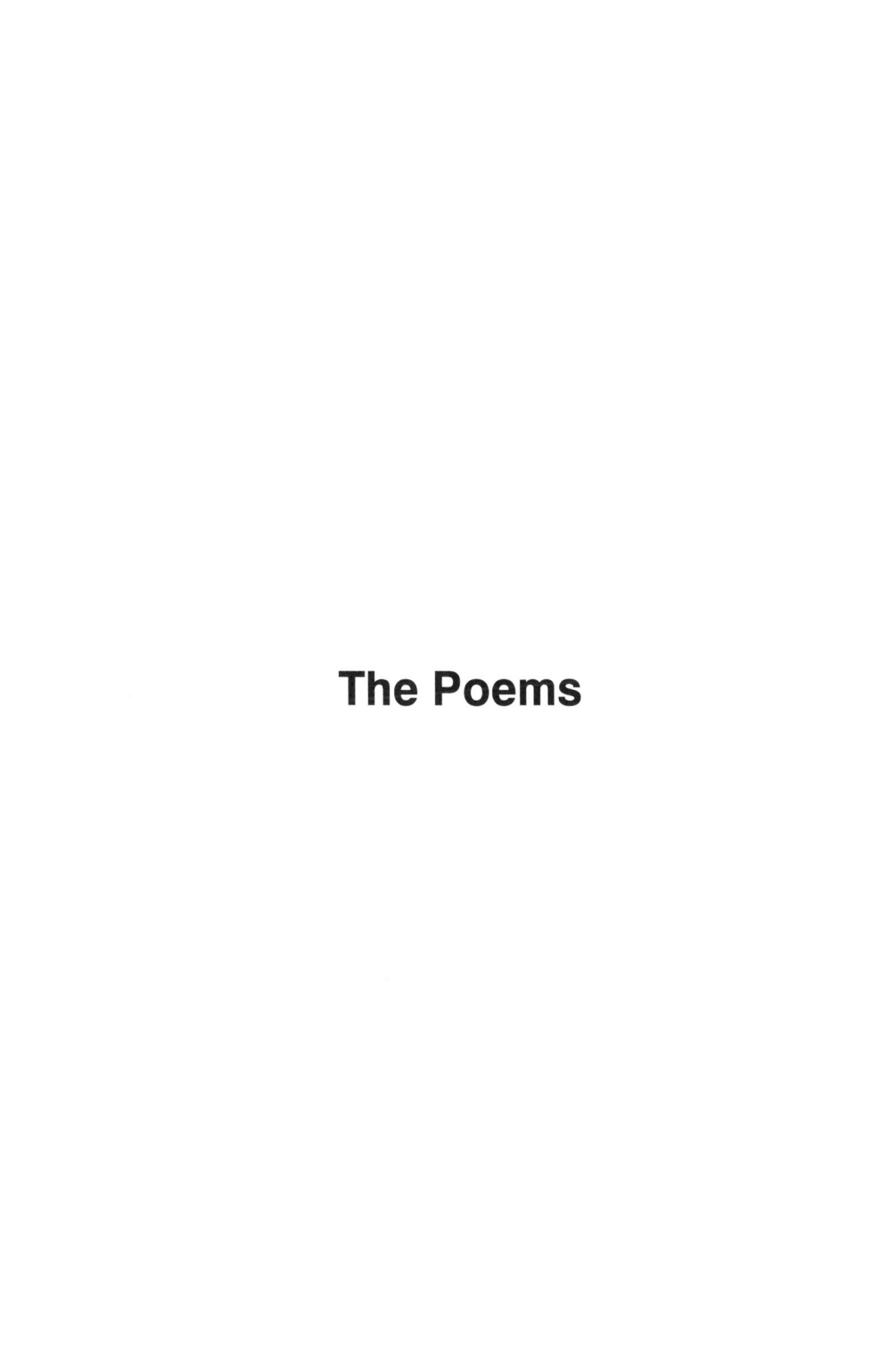

Ginger

My hamster's name is Ginger,
Because he is that colour,
He likes to run on his wheel
And he loves to drink water,
He likes to sleep a lot too.

Connor Hunter (8)
Clepington Primary School, Dundee

Woof!

My name is Rocky, I drive Shannon mad,
Sometimes I make Shannon sad,
But I don't mean to be bad,
Dad, Dad, Dad oh when will you be home,
To give me a lovely bone?

Shannon Millar (8)
Clepington Primary School, Dundee

Rusty

I have a dog, Rusty,
She can be funny,
She has a friend Dusty
And I love her and feed her.

My dog Rusty is brown,
She can be weird at times,
Rusty likes to go to town
And she likes to play.

Rusty is not allowed to come to school,
She can go crazy,
Because she barks and that's not cool
And at the end of the day she sleeps
And that's my dog Rusty.

Laura Milton (8)
Clepington Primary School, Dundee

My Pet

I have a little tortoise
And he doesn't make noise,
He has lettuce and cucumber to eat,
He has tiny squashy feet.

Harley Martin (8)
Clepington Primary School, Dundee

My Cat

I've got a cat and his name is Tom,
I've got a cat and he often goes mad,
I've got a cat and he's so cute,
I've got a cat and dogs are scared!

I've got a cat and he begs a lot,
I've got a cat and he plays with me,
I've got a cat and he watches me,
I've got a cat and he sleeps a lot!

Tony Williamson (8)
Clepington Primary School, Dundee

My Cat Karma

Karma is my cat and she is mine,
Karma is my cat and she is fine,
Karma is my cat, she has a favourite ball,
She plays with it every day on the floor.

Karma is my cat and she is fine,
Karma is my cat and she is mine,
I like her and she likes me,
So she hugs me,
She plays with everyone.

Rebecca McColl (8)
Clepington Primary School, Dundee

My Favourite Animal

My auntie has a dog who barks a lot,
With white and browny spots,
He looks like a meat eater,
But he really is not.

He holds his paw up for you to take,
He is a lovely dog,
I give him lots of dog food
And take him out for walks.

Amy Gallacher (8)
Clepington Primary School, Dundee

Dundee's Law

On the hill of Dundee,
Where the sun always shines,
Where the extinct volcano
Sleeps at night.

The stars are out,
The stars will shine,
Use the peace you have tonight.

I love Dundee,
I love its sight,
Come together, let's unite.

Robbie Norrie (11)
Clepington Primary School, Dundee

Problems

Problems, problems, problems, so many problems,
Global warming is a problem all over the world,
The ice caps will soon be no more,
It's true, we all know the score.

Problems, problems, so many problems,
Poverty is a problem all over the world,
Poor people have to put up with the street,
To get a job would be a great feat.

Problems, problems, problems, so many problems,
War is a problem all over the world,
The soldiers leave their country to serve,
But none of these things they really deserve.

Lewis MacLaughlan (11)
Clepington Primary School, Dundee

The Sandwich

The sandwich I like is nice and white
And is usually very bright
And the one I like is full of Marmite
That's the one I like to bite.

Dean Imlay (11)
Clepington Primary School, Dundee

Scotland

I can see the spectacular views,
From the top of the mountain.

I can feel the squelchy grass,
Below me from the top of the mountain.

I can smell the beautiful scent
Of the purple heather from
The top of the mountain.

I can taste the crisp air,
Blowing on me from the top of the mountain.

I hear the tweeting of the birds
From the top of the mountain.

I love the views, the grass,
The smells, the air and the birds,
From the top of the mountain.

Sarah Green (11)
Clepington Primary School, Dundee

My Gran

My gran, Maureen is her name,
She died on the 10th of May,
She lived in England, way down south,
I used to visit her in the house,
She was in a hospice for about a week,
She had cancer and she was very weak,
She was on a machine that kept her alive,
But after a week she had had enough
And she wanted to die,
My gran, a super woman she was,
I think about her every day,
But I know she is still with me
And she will be proud of me every day
Until the day I die.

Reece McArtney (11)
Clepington Primary School, Dundee

Me!

I am as tall as a statue,
As loud as speakers
And as jumpy as space hoppers,
Oh and as happy as cheerleaders,
Also as Scottish as Scotland
And as bananas as bananas,
Also as fast as a tiger.

Aled Bartley-Jones (11)
Clepington Primary School, Dundee

Happy New Year

H opefully you will work very well,
A lot of fun,
P lease be nice to everyone,
P arty with people,
Y ou are the best.

N obody is going to harm you,
E xcited,
W ill you be a good helper?

Y ahoo!
E xtremely beautiful,
A ll people say you are flexible,
R eady for brilliance.

John Joe Fitzpatrick (10)
Clepington Primary School, Dundee

Friends

If you'd be my friend . . .
I'd float into space
And I'd slap my face,
I'd jump off monkey bars,
Then fly to Mars.

I would kiss a deer
And jump off a pier,
I'd eat a jellyfish
And lick a dirty dish.

I'd die my hair purple
And eat a turtle,
I'd eat soggy hay,
In the middle of the day.

Jump off a cliff,
A stinky shoe I'd sniff
And smile without end,
If you'd be my friend.

Henna Saleem (10)
Clepington Primary School, Dundee

Without You

Without you I'm like a beach
With no sand,
A book with no words,
Or a guitarist with no hand.

Without you I'm like the sun
With no heat,
A rainbow with no colour,
Or a bong with no beat.

James Glover (10)
Clepington Primary School, Dundee

Friends

If you'd be my friend,
I'd break my legs,
Eat rotten eggs,
Smell some toes,
Break my nose,
Wet my bed,
Eat my friend called Ted
And smile without end,
If you'd be my friend.

Aarron Lee Donaldson (11)
Clepington Primary School, Dundee

Friends

If you'd be my friend,
I'd cover myself in bread,
Throw away my bed,
Eat a pile of hay,
Play football all day.

Throw myself into a cow pat,
Eat a live furry bat,
I'd eat a soggy old bun
And never have any fun
And smile without end,
If you'd be my friend!

Rachel Tonelli (10)
Clepington Primary School, Dundee

It's As Easy As . . .

It's as easy as this,
It's as easy as that,
It's as easy as training a totally wild bat,
It's as easy as turning your eyes to brown,
It's as easy as changing up to down,
It's as easy as making a snail go fast,
It's as easy as making a sweet forever last,
It's as easy as turning a crocodile yellow,
It's as easy as playing the great big cello,
It's as easy as making a guitar out of rubber,
It's as easy as taking off the walrus' blubber,
It's as easy as this, it's no piece of cake,
Trying to get rid of my toffee toothache!

Lauren McIntosh (10)
Clepington Primary School, Dundee

Friends

If you'd be my friend . . .

I'd swim with sharks,
Give off sparks,
Jump off a cliff,
A smelly shoe I'd sniff,
Jump to the moon,
Be a baboon,
Paint myself red,
Wet the bed,
Ballet dance all day,
Then bathe in clay,
Travel to space,
Live in a case,
My love wouldn't end,
If you'd be my friend.

Kirsty Jane Gallacher (10)
Clepington Primary School, Dundee

Friends

If you'd be my friend . . .

I'd run a hard race,
Float into space,
Eat a small tree,
Drink from the sea,
Write all day,
Having nothing to say,
Eat some glue,
Sniff a smelly shoe
And smile without end,
If you'd be my friend.

Rachael Strachan (10)
Clepington Primary School, Dundee

Friends

If you'd be my friend,
I'd paint myself red,
Wet my bed,
Fly to Mars,
Bang my head on monkey bars,
Jump off a cliff,
A smelly shoe I'll sniff,
Cut off my hair,
Run about in my underwear
And smile without end,
If you'd be my friend!

Rhys Mackenzie (10)
Clepington Primary School, Dundee

Friend!

If you'd be my friend!

I'd eat mouldy bread,
Dye my hair red,
Lick a cat,
Sit on a mat,
Sniff a smelly shoe
And eat a poo,
Cut all my hair,
Fall off my chair,
Pick my nose,
Chew on my toes
And smile without end,
If you'd be my friend.

Eilidh Richardson (10)
Clepington Primary School, Dundee

Without You

Without you,
I'm like a pencil without lead,
I'm like a computer without a screen,
Or a mattress without a bed.

Without you I'm like some flowers without water,
For whatever I do, you always understand.

Ali Mahmood (10)
Clepington Primary School, Dundee

Eyes

My eyes are shimmering blue
As the beautiful sea swaying side to side,
Blue as a sparkling sapphire
And scattered with white,
White as my school polo shirt,
White as my handkerchief.

Cameron Healy (10)
Clepington Primary School, Dundee

Friends

If you'll be my friend . . .

I'll jump off a cliff,
Eat jellyfish,
I'll paint myself red,
Wet my bed,
I'll kill my fish
And play with a smelly, mouldy dish,
Walk off a pier
And kiss a deer,
Eat Mars bars,
Fly to Mars,
I'll eat smelly hay,
In the middle of May,
Cut off all my long blonde hair,
Run around in my underwear
And smile without end,
If you'll be my friend.

Kayleigh Brough (10)
Clepington Primary School, Dundee

One Amazing Football Match!

The fans walking down the road,
Singing their hearts out with joy,
The excitement waiting for your team
To come out onto the pitch,
The crusty hot mince pies at half-time,
The joy that my team is winning!

Kieran Sturrock (10)
Clepington Primary School, Dundee

The Carnival

A merry-go-round with pretty red horses
Riding around and around,
Cheerful children on the big bouncy bungee jumpers,
That leap up in the air,
Beefy hot dogs sizzling noisily on the hot grill,
The fluffy pink candyfloss that sticks to my fingers.

Morgan Ann Low (11)
Clepington Primary School, Dundee

Oh Wonderful Beach

Wonderful water coming to the sand,
Super waves whispering to me,
Soggy sand on the beach,
My sandwich is going cold.

Billy West (10)
Clepington Primary School, Dundee

The Beach

Big silver jagged rocks at the beach,
Waves going so smoothly, gliding along the way,
The breezy air in the sky,
Hot golden sand tickling my toes,
Chocolate ice cream melting in my hand.

Abbie Taylor (11)
Clepington Primary School, Dundee

The Library

Dusty books, stacked upon the shelf,
Silence, from all around the room,
Fresh cups of tea, straight from the boiling kettle,
Concentration, all around me.

Hannah Scott
Clepington Primary School, Dundee

My Holiday

Creamy white caravans sitting in the sun,
Swerving white seagulls stamping on the caravans,
Gluey rich candyfloss sticking to my face,
Smooth gleaming warm grass running through my feet,
I love this place!

Astrid Vaughan (10)
Clepington Primary School, Dundee

The Garden

Golden sunshine beaming down on the dull green leaves,
Soft rustle of the cheeky little birds gathering their tea,
Sweet-smelling flowers sitting gorgeously under the delicate
Glare of the evening light,
The calm breeze gliding through my smooth hair.

Jessica Ross (10)
Clepington Primary School, Dundee

My Room

Old damaged books, grey and dull,
Hanging out at the front of my bed,
Cheesy socks all over the place,
Under the bed, everywhere!
Speedy spiders knock at my door,
Scuttering about on the floor,
The lumpy mattress bouncing up and down,
Like a roller coaster nightmare.

Chloe Teale (10)
Clepington Primary School, Dundee

The River Tay

Friendly dolphins jumping in the air,
Angry waves crashing on the pebbles,
Fresh, salty, windy air blowing past me,
Golden gentle sand in-between your toes.

Jared Duncan (10)
Clepington Primary School, Dundee

At The Seaside

Rocks glimmering in the sunshine,
The waves rushing back and forth behind me,
The slimy seaweed that's washed up by the waves,
The sand getting in-between my toes
And tickling my feet,
Oh the seaside!

Callum Wood (10)
Clepington Primary School, Dundee

Football

Supporters with angry faces,
Shouting from the big crowd,
Hot greasy pies from the baker's van,
Joy from all the big football fans,
Goal!

Lee Kerr (10)
Clepington Primary School, Dundee

The Library

Hundreds of books in the quiet library,
Keyboards clicking peacefully away,
Quiet, pleasant air everywhere,
A shiny book by Roald Dahl in my hand.

David West (10)
Clepington Primary School, Dundee

My Chip Shop

The busy chip shop at the top of my street,
Hungry people talking about their day at work,
Hot chips that burn my mouth,
Delicious salt and vinegar -
Mmm tasty!
That's my chip shop.

Lee Collins (10)
Clepington Primary School, Dundee

Football Crazy

Dark blue Dundee logos,
Upon my team's shirt,
Foul language from the
Angry, freezing fans,
Cheesy chips at half-time,
Excitement for the golden goals,
Hot chocolate at the end of the tireful day.

John Shields (10)
Clepington Primary School, Dundee

Sticks

The sticks battering the ball,
The sticks clanging against each other,
Sweat on the players,
Tiredness!
I've run too much!

Iain Cunningham (11)
Clepington Primary School, Dundee

The Football Match

A football match,
It's amazing as it could be,
Strong bad language and dirty words,
Mince pies in the hot oven, so very tasty,
Jumping up to score a goal -
And they do!

Rafiq Shakeel (11)
Clepington Primary School, Dundee

Curry

Spicy Indian curry on the pan,
People saying yum-yum
When it comes on the table,
Curry in my throat
Makes my nose run.

Aadam Un-Nabi (10)
Clepington Primary School, Dundee

The Beach

Sparkling shells laying in the hot sand,
Silent waves sweeping back into the sea,
Chocolate ice cream melting in my hands,
Golden sand running through my toes.

Zahira Yasin (10)
Clepington Primary School, Dundee

The Car Boot Sale

Lots of gleaming cars,
Lots of people at the car boot sale,
Dunkin' Donuts in a big truck,
Tables covered with toys.

Sinead McDonagh (10)
Clepington Primary School, Dundee

The Sales

Shops vandalised with sale signs in the castle-sized mall,
People darting into crowded shops with big, heavy bags,
Coffee sitting on a dirty table in the café,
Exciting feelings running down my bony spine,
My sandwich travels down a roller coaster to my hungry belly,
Must get back to those sales now.

Lucy Hendry (10)
Clepington Primary School, Dundee

My Gran

My gran says there's no such as a gift on someone's birthday
The thought of wishing them counts,
My gran says there's no need to wear special clothes for a party,
The thought of going counts,
My gran says there's no need for a gift on Mother's Day,
The thought of giving her big hugs counts.

I wonder if my gran is serious,
I wonder sometimes.

Aisha Mahmood (11)
Clepington Primary School, Dundee

My Dad's Birthday

I see my dad enjoying himself,
I touch my bottle as I am about to drink it,
I hear people singing Happy Birthday to him,
I smell the birthday cake in the distance,
I taste a bit of the cake,
It is delicious.
Happy Birthday!

Darren Pake (11)
Clepington Primary School, Dundee

The Sky

The sky is blue,
The clouds are white,
When there is thunder,
I get a fright!

Megan Lorimer (11)
Clepington Primary School, Dundee

The Great Wall

I see the amazing views of the Great Wall,
I hear the birds singing beautifully,
I feel the heat burning my skin,
I taste the spices in the air,
I smell the fresh air blowing in the wind,
I'd love to go there again.

Kerri Corstorphine (11)
Clepington Primary School, Dundee

About Me!

I am as small as an ant,
Big as a tower,
Thin as a pin,
Thick as a tree trunk,
Bold as a blackboard,
But that is just me.

Chloe Davidson (11)
Clepington Primary School, Dundee

The Bus People

The bus is a huge metal monster,
It drives people around the town,
It sometimes stops at the dumpster,
They are mainly driven by a stuntman,
Bang, bang goes the engine,
Sit down or you're off with no money back,
Secretly it's not really a public transport,
It's really a thief organisation for your money,
That's why they never stop at your proper destination.

Lewis Chalmers (11)
Clepington Primary School, Dundee

When My Hamster Died!

When my hamster died,
I was very sad, I cried
And now I know,
That my pet is fast asleep
And will never be with me!

Heather Heenan (11)
Clepington Primary School, Dundee

Dundee's Weather

Oh Dundee, what a town,
The weather often makes me frown,
The leaves are scattered,
The trees are bare,
Tell me,
Why is the snow no longer here?
Is it because it's no longer there?
The ice caps are melting,
Creatures almost extinct,
Tell me,
What can we do to bring back,
Such a beautiful thing?

Josh Anderson (11)
Clepington Primary School, Dundee

Friends

F unny and nice,
R eally good at games,
I n my school,
E very day we play football,
N ot a lot of footballs,
D id you guess?
S ometimes we play lots of made up games.

Kieran Philp (11)
Clepington Primary School, Dundee

The Arrival Of A New Baby

My heart was pounding,
My face was glistening with sweat,
I heard the phone ring,
I stood up and ran to the phone,
It's a boy! I always wanted a little brother,
I have one now, I'm a big sister now,
I could jump for joy.

Anisah Ahmed (11)
Clepington Primary School, Dundee

Roller Coaster Ride

The suspense was growing,
As I was in the queue,
For the world's biggest roller coaster.

I was so excited that my legs
Started to tremble,
I was so, so excited.

As I pulled the safety rail over my head,
The roller coaster moved slowly.

Then it went so fast that my hair went everywhere.

That was the best day I had out with my friends.

Iona Boath (11)
Clepington Primary School, Dundee

Not Me

I am me,
I'll never change,
No matter what,
Even when I pop my clogs,
I'll still be me in my world.

You are you, just now,
You might change later,
I won't,
You can change from bad to good
Or good to bad but I won't know.

Whilst you're busy changing from
One thing to another,
I'll be here, following my dreams,
Being me.

Zoe Blackwood
Clepington Primary School, Dundee

Mum

Awesome manners
Great planner
Child lover
My mother
Good listener
Brilliant whistler
Real spoiler
Warm boiler
Treat bringer
Lovely singer
Make-up wearer
Brilliant darer
Sensible drinker
Great thinker.

Katie Strachan (9)
Crombie Primary School, Crombie

If

If my friend was a flower,
She'd be a bright red rose,
Warm and romantic
And sometimes a little bit thorny.

If my friend was an animal,
She'd be a brown, fluffy monkey,
Cheeky, friendly and mischievous
And always full of energy.

If my friend was a season,
She'd be a hot, orange summer,
Bright and orange
And very warm and reassuring.

If my friend was a chocolate,
She'd be a mouth-melting Malteser,
Soft and so dreamy on the inside,
But strong on the outside.

Isla McLeod (10)
Crombie Primary School, Crombie

Without You
(To my nana)

Without you I'm like a planet with no sun,
I'm like a sky with no birds
Or a mouth with no tongue.

Without you I'm like a fish without sea,
I'm like a rainbow with no colours,
Please come back to me.

Cameron Montgomery (9)
Crombie Primary School, Crombie

Holly

Good swimmer
Badge winner
Plant carer
Good sharer
Book reader
Brilliant leader
Good planner
Lovely manners
Cat feeder
Fun pleader
Bike rider
Big strider
Gymnastics master
Can run faster
Good knitter
Dog sitter.

Kayleigh Hood (9)
Crombie Primary School, Crombie

If

If my dad was a firework,
He would be a rocket,
With a loud, big bang,
Then he'd come back to the ground.

If my dad was an animal,
He would be a tiger,
Protecting his young
And pouncing on his prey.

If my dad was a clown,
He would make everybody laugh
And hop everywhere and have fun
And play games with me all day.

AJ Burns (9)
Crombie Primary School, Crombie

Baby Brother

Milk drinker
Wondrous thinker
Good listener
Non whistler
Likes to slather
Will get clever
Silent sleeper
Big peepers
Likes to yell
As loud as a bell
Loud crier
Has a pacifier.

Liam Campbell (11)
Crombie Primary School, Crombie

If

If my mum was a dessert,
She'd be a chocolate sundae,
Mouth-watering and delicious
And good enough to eat.

If my mum was a colour,
She'd be sparkling white,
Like snow in the winter,
Or like clouds in the sky.

If my mum was a drink,
She'd be bubbly wine,
In a crystal glass,
To drink so fine.

If my mum was an animal,
She'd be a great big hawk,
Grabbing and clenching,
Protecting her young.

Kyle Smith (11)
Crombie Primary School, Crombie

Without You
(To my best friend)

Without you I'm like a God without creation,
I'm like a sun with no light
Or a head without imagination.

Without you I'm like a workbook with no improvement,
I'm like a cut that doesn't heal,
Or a swing without movement.

Holly Roxburgh (9)
Crombie Primary School, Crombie

Mrs Birrell (My Teacher)

Pupil carer
No one fairer
Story reader
Sweet feeder
Work marker
Book parker
Lipstick wearer
News sharer
Mistake maker
Work taker
Best teacher
Never a screecher.

Toni Marshall (9)
Crombie Primary School, Crombie

Blue

Inside the forest's green coating,
The parrots sing their song
And you will find them silky blue,
With a tail that's so long.

A delicate blue sapphire,
Shimmering in the sun,
You can't just get them every day,
They're sparkly and fun.

A fluttering blue butterfly,
All colourful and bright,
When summer goes and autumn comes,
The light turns into night.

A blue pansy in the garden,
Its petals spreading wide,
The perfume's close around this place,
Just like the sea's blue tide.

Kate Schafferius (10)
Crombie Primary School, Crombie

Jaguars

Large, spotty, yellow cat,
Quiet, sneaky, peaceful,
He leaps through the jungle,
Purrs, sleeps,
Predator.

Paige Gardner (11)
Inverkeithing Primary School, Inverkeithing

What My Feeling!

When I am down, I go yellow,
When I am angry, I go red,
When I am alone, I go black
And when I am happy, I go multicoloured,
When I go white, I am bored,
When I go cold, I go blue.

I like writing in multicoloured,
It makes the page look nice.

And when the teachers are angry,
They all have fire coming out of their ears.

Francesca McShane (11)
Inverkeithing Primary School, Inverkeithing

A Purple Dragon

Three heads,
Three evil brains,
Six red eyes,
One scaly body,
Five razor-sharp horns,
Four powerful wings,
Twelve enormous legs,
Two grabbling arms,
Nine slimy tongues,
Thousands of blood-covered spikes,
Twenty-two lashing tails,
Nineteen years old,
Eats meat.

Wayne Bridges (11)
Inverkeithing Primary School, Inverkeithing

Puppies

P uppies like to play with me,
U se ball, bones and lots more,
P uppies are as cute as anything,
P uppies are happy to see and
P lay with someone,
Y ou and me both know
   And think they are so, so cute.

Melissa Black (11)
Inverkeithing Primary School, Inverkeithing

Drugs

When up on that hill,
You need a pill,
You know what to do,
Start a new life with some kids and a wife,
Get a job, get a life,
You know what to do.

Shaun Smith (11)
Inverkeithing Primary School, Inverkeithing

Stella The Fairy

Stella is the fairy of the stars,
She just can't fly very far,
Her left wing is weak,
She is also timid and is meek,
She has golden hair like the sun
And she knows how to have fun,
She likes to have parties with her friends
And in Fairy Tale Land the fun never ends!
She has to attend Fairy Tale School,
But with all its trips, it really is cool!
Her best fairy friend is May,
They laugh and fly all day!

Abby Drummond (11)
Inverkeithing Primary School, Inverkeithing

TV

TV rocks!
TV is cool!
I always watch it when I come home from school,
Soaps, comedy, drama and sci-fi,
It's all on the digital box called Sky,
Freeview, Sky, Sky+ and HD,
They are too many, it confuses me.

Disney Channel is so great,
I always watch it from 7 till 8,
There are twins that live in a hotel,
They make other's lives feel like Hell,
Hannah the pop star is totally fantastic,
In the movie 'Mean Girls' there is a group called The Plastics,
Now you know why TV is great,
I bet you'll watch it and you can't wait.

Gemma Park (11)
Inverkeithing Primary School, Inverkeithing

Hard Times

Hard times look very dangerous,
Hard times look like being plunged into darkness,
Hard times sound like belts whipping off children.

Hard times sound like babies crying,
Hard times feel like you aren't wanted.

Hard times feel like you want to die with anger,
I feel like running away but I can't.

Kourtney Lyness (10)
Inverkeithing Primary School, Inverkeithing

Hard Times

Hard times look grey and all I see is,
White sun in my head.

I look over bleakness and my eyes
Gaze over chimneys.

Hard times sound like machines buzzing,
I hear the noise of banging on the door.

My ears only hear a booming noise,
I listen to the machines.

Hard times feel lonely and scary,
I feel my heart thumping,
My feelings are only of fear.

Sarah Clouston (10)
Inverkeithing Primary School, Inverkeithing

Hard Times

Hard times look very crowded,
Dusty, black and very, very smelly,
Hard times look like there is no food for my family and others,
Everywhere you look there are rats all over the place.

Hard times sound like machines buzzing around in my head,
Hard times sound like my master shouting at me,
My friends trying to keep their screams in,
But from far away you can hear them still.

Hard times feel like I'm going to be sick,
I have butterflies in my stomach,
I want to go away but I'm too scared.

Toni-Leigh Watson (10)
Inverkeithing Primary School, Inverkeithing

Hard Times

The hard times look like,
A crowded street,
Black windows,
The cobbled street
And it has smoke from the chimneys.

Alexander Sinclair (11)
Inverkeithing Primary School, Inverkeithing

Hard Times

Like a black, scary night,
    And a crack,
        The smack.
There is someone in the darkness,
    Echoing like a crack,
        The smack.
Fear - rolling myself up,
    Sick when I was sick,
The man came closer and I said,
    'Go away mister,' and he said,
        'No!'
And I ran away.

John Mitchell (10)
Inverkeithing Primary School, Inverkeithing

Hard Times

Hard times are so lonely, so dull, so hard,
I feel anger towards the people who are rich.

The noise is echoing through my ears,
It just doesn't go away.

When I come home to my grey house,
I look back to see if someone is coming,
But all I see is blackness.

Christopher Ostrom (10)
Inverkeithing Primary School, Inverkeithing

Hard Times

Hard times look dull and dark,
Crowded with people,
Dusty everywhere about me,
Lonely all by myself.

Hard times sound loud,
The fire crackling,
The echoing of people shouting,
People thumping their feet.

Hard times feel sick,
People are tired,
Children feel hungry
And very angry.

Lorna Forker (10)
Inverkeithing Primary School, Inverkeithing

Hard Times

Hard times look shameful, cruel sometimes,
Sad and sore,
Some people think it's good, some bad,
Even though hard times are hard,
Hard times sound like my master screaming at me,
Most of the time sounds scary because of machines,
Hard times feel like stinging eyes,
Because of the soot in my eyes.

Dylan Hall (10)
Inverkeithing Primary School, Inverkeithing

Hard Times

I was in the street when I looked at the sky
And all of the sky was dark grey.

And when I looked at the sky I saw the sun
But it wasn't bright yellow,
It was very grey,
Like the clouds and the smoke from
The big, huge factory.

Every time I got the whip I hated that
Sound like a snap on my back and
My bare hands.

When my mum died and then my dad died too,
I wanted to die as well and when I light the fire,
I feel unhappy.

Kayleigh Fosker (10)
Inverkeithing Primary School, Inverkeithing

Jelly

Wibbly wobbly jelly,
Sitting on my plate,
Sweet, fruity jelly,
Delicious to eat.
Huge, smells wonderful,
All different colours,
Pink, purple, red, yellow,
Green, orange and blue,
Enjoyable to eat,
Have it with ice cream,
Have it with strawberries,
I like fruity jelly,
Cold, fresh jelly,
It trickles down your throat,
Slippery, sloppy, slimy,
Mushy, tasty, sweet,
Fruity, lovely, soothing,
Wibbly wobbly jelly.

Emilly Campbell (10)
Inverkeithing Primary School, Inverkeithing

Food

Tasty, colourful, yummy,
The smell of it makes you feel hungry,
Sweet, strong, sour,
It melts in your mouth,
Thanks to animals, we have food,
Great Britain, France, Italy,
All countries have their different foods,
Pasta, pizza, cakes,
They all have their tastes,
Strawberries, satsumas, berries,
They taste good and they're healthy,
Food is a rainbow,
It is the best thing on Earth.

Claire Fairbairn (10)
Inverkeithing Primary School, Inverkeithing

Parents

Happy, fun, always kind,
Caring, helpful, sometimes strict,
Take care of you in lots of different ways,
Great at helping when you're hurt,
Parents are gentle and they don't hit,
Not always angry, only when they shout,
They always look after you,
Always tidy and not silly.

Parents take care of you in the right way,
Sensible, brilliant, encouraging and not scary,
Perfect at helping and being angels,
Sometimes teach you when you're young,
Sometimes really sad but mostly friendly,
It does not matter they're your parents,
They are the best thing ever.

Stuart Milne (10)
Inverkeithing Primary School, Inverkeithing

Babies

Babies scream, babies crawl,
Babies are really small,
Babies are always in the mood,
To eat some really mushy food,
Babies start off really small,
Then they grow up really tall,
Babies always wear nappies,
Then go to the room with the tappies,
Finally when they're tall,
They have someone really small.

Daniel Sinclair (10)
Inverkeithing Primary School, Inverkeithing

My Sister Ashton

Playful, happy, sad,
Fast, slow, funny,
As fast as a charging bull
And as funny as a clown,
Cheerful, nasty, kind,
Quiet, loud, sneaky,
Sometimes as quiet as a mouse,
Hungry, sleepy,
She is as hungry as a lion
And as sleepy as a sloth sleeping.

Kieran Gear (10)
Inverkeithing Primary School, Inverkeithing

My Name

C olz is my nickname,
O pal Fruits are my favourite,
L ove doing athletics, it's the best,
I want to be a champion boxer,
N iloc is my name backwards.

L aughing and talking all the time,
A lways having a great time with my friends,
W ith my dog named Jet.

Colin Law (10)
Inverkeithing Primary School, Inverkeithing

The Rainforest

The rainforest is dark, cold at night,
But day is hot and misty,
South America has big rainforests,
That are getting chopped down!
The rainforest, full of trees,
That provide Earth's oxygen,
Because rainforests are being chopped down,
Animals are losing precious homes,
If you are in the rainforest,
You'll get lost pretty easily,
More people die these days,
Because the rainforest is dying,
Rainforest, red with colours,
Turning different by the minute,
The rainforest is like,
A bag full of different leaves,
Red, yellow and brown,
Are the rainforest's different colours,
The rainforest is,
A jungle when you're in it,
The rainforest is scary,
When you are on your own,
Some of the rainforest trees
Are gnarled like a twisted rope you cannot undo,
Trees are so tall in the rainforest,
That you cannot see the top,
The rainforest is so green,
It looks like you're looking at a clump of grass,
In the rainforest the rain is so heavy,
That you could get drowned within the hour.

Christopher Naughton (10)
Inverkeithing Primary School, Inverkeithing

The Writer Of This Poem
(Based on 'The Writer of this Poem' by Roger McGough)

The writer of this poem,
Is as big as a tree,
As strong as a rhino,
As gentle as a fly.

As fast as a car,
As slow as a turtle,
As happy as a clown,
As silly as a monkey.

As big as a hippo,
As loud as an elephant,
As dumb as a dumpling,
As good as a fairy.

Kiera Pick (9)
Lynburn Primary School, Dunfermline

Pink

Pink is petals on a rose,
Pink is the Playboy
Bunny on your clothes
And pink makes the
Boys wink and pink
Is the sound of my
Singing pillow, singing
On my bed,
Pink is a pink necklace box
And the sound of a
Jewellery box singing
And pink earrings in my ears
And my necklace hanging from my neck.
Pink.

Jamie-Lee Curran (9)
Lynburn Primary School, Dunfermline

Rose Who Picked Her Nose

There was a naughty girl named Rose,
Who always picked her great big nose,
One day she got her finger stuck up the great big thing
And then she got stuck in a hospital wing,
She got operated on but did not wake again,
Due to damage to the brain.

Sean Birrell (9)
Lynburn Primary School, Dunfermline

The Writer Of This Poem
(Based on 'The Writer of this Poem' by Roger McGough)

The writer of this poem,
Is big for his age,
As strong as a pro wrestler,
As gentle as a cat.

As fast as a car,
As slow as a snail,
As happy as a bunny,
As silly as a clown.

As funny as can be,
As odd as a sum,
As busy as a bee you see
And now it's time to go, hee, hee, hee.

Jacob Stephenson (9)
Lynburn Primary School, Dunfermline

Pink

Pink is a lipstick
And it's bright,
Pink is a rose and
Blossom outside,
Pink is a limo and nice,
Pink is happy and
The colour is nice,
Pink can be a colour for a top,
Pink can be a kind of milkshake,
Pink can be a colour for a jewellery box,
Pink is a great colour, it looks nice.

Kayleigh Anne Lindsell (9)
Lynburn Primary School, Dunfermline

Sean Clover

There was a man called Sean Clover,
Who always ran people over,
The police came one day
And took him away,
They put him behind bars
And that stopped him driving fast cars.

Billy-John Jack (9)
Lynburn Primary School, Dunfermline

Sleepy Ryan

There once was a boy called Sleepy Ryan,
He just lay there like a lazy lion,
Then one day the fire bell went,
He could not hear, he was in his tent,
He was cuddling into his ted
And the firemen found him dead.

Sean David Wilson (9)
Lynburn Primary School, Dunfermline

The Writer Of This Poem
(Based on 'The Writer of this Poem' by Roger McGough)

The writer of this poem,
Is a little thin man,
As strong as Bruce Lee,
As gentle as a little genie,
As stupid as a clown.

As fast as Formula 1,
As slow as a snail,
As happy as Ronaldinho,
As silly as a drunk guy.

As funny as a circus,
As forgetful as my gran,
As dumb as a dog,
As quiet as a mouse.

As good as a teacher.

Peter McKean (10)
Lynburn Primary School, Dunfermline

Kenny Ate A Penny!

There was a naughty, stupid boy called Kenny,
Who always sucked on pennies,
He swallowed a penny that tasted like wood,
This naughty, stupid boy was in such a bad mood,
Too many pennies hurt his big head,
Now stupid Kenny is dead.

Kerri-Jade Todd (9)
Lynburn Primary School, Dunfermline

Yellow

Yellow are daffodils,
Blowing in the fields,
Yellow is the sun,
Shining very bright,
Happiness in the summertime,
Yellow sand,
At the sunny beach,
Drinking banana milkshake,
Beside the Red Sea,
Yellow canaries,
Tweeting in the trees,
Royal antelopes running in the breeze,
Time to go now, bye-bye, let's go home before it snows.

Carly Westwater & Chloe Foster (9)
Lynburn Primary School, Dunfermline

The Writer Of This Poem
(Based on 'The Writer of this Poem' by Roger McGough)

The writer of this poem,
Is as hungry as a monkey,
As strong as a mouse,
As gentle as a starfish.

As fast as a cheetah,
As slow as a wish,
As happy as the sun,
As silly as a clown.

As bright as fire,
As deep as the ocean,
As dry as a pancake,
As busy as a bee.

Danielle Lafferty (9)
Lynburn Primary School, Dunfermline

The Controller Tragedy

There was a boy named Dexter Fox,
He couldn't take his eyes off his Xbox,
It was a very terrible sight,
If someone said *Boo*, he wouldn't get a fright,
His mum and dad sent him to bed,
But he turned on his Xbox instead,
His mum and dad got a fright,
Because his eyes turned square with all their might,
He never ate his food as his mum said,
Soon he was dead.

Fraser Wilson & Ryan Colbert (9)
Lynburn Primary School, Dunfermline

A Girl Called Rose

There was a nice girl called Rose,
Who always just picked her nose,
She put her finger up so far,
That she felt like a star,
Then one day she felt so ill,
She dropped dead on the floor very still.

Sean Carroll (9)
Lynburn Primary School, Dunfermline

Light

Light is the sun rising in the east,
Light is the stars sparkling in the beautiful sky at night,
Light is the glowing fire on a wintry night,
Light is a moon that shines brightly in the sky,
Light is the lava in the lamp that sparkles in the room,
Light helps us to see,
Light is the torch guiding me to happiness,
Light is the glow stick dancing on the wall,
Light is the nightlight protecting me from the dark,
Light is the headlamps glowing from the car,
Light is the love that makes us happy,
Life is light.

Rachel Timmins (9)
St John the Baptist Primary School, Fauldhouse

The Light

Light is a glowing fire on a wintry night,
Light is a lava lamp making bubbly shapes,
Light is the reflection of the sun setting over the sea,
Light is when love first begins,
Light is summer when it bursts into season,
Light is a glow stick dancing on a wall,
Jesus is the Light of the world.

Colette Rowell (9)
St John the Baptist Primary School, Fauldhouse

The Light

Light is the fire that guides me in the forest,
Light is the happiness of my achievements,
Light is the happiness of a newborn baby,
Light is the love of a marriage,
Light is the reflection of the moon,
Light is the beginning of a new life,
Light is being a part of God's family,
Light is the twinkle of a star,
Light is the sign of happiness,
We are the light of the world,
Children are tomorrow's people.

Jordan McCormick (9)
St John the Baptist Primary School, Fauldhouse

Light

Light is my nightlight protecting me from darkness,
Light is the sun shining through the day,
Light is the moon reflecting the beautiful sun,
Light is Superglue keeping my eyes open in the day,
Light is God watching us in the day and night,
Light is the path to get into Heaven,
Light is the pathway to the future,
Light is my lava lamp making beautiful shapes,
Light is the moon reflecting the shining sun,
Light is the joy of someone's wedding party,
Light is the sun reflecting water to make a rainbow,
Light is the oil lamps that the miners used down in the coal mines,
Peace in the world is beautiful light.

Munro McKay (9)
St John the Baptist Primary School, Fauldhouse

Light

Light is the sun shining on me when I am sunbathing,
Light is a smile on my face when I am happy,
Light is a heart that is burning with love,
Light is a kiss when you're getting married,
Light is a rainbow of happiness,
Light is a woman that cries when her baby is born safely,
My family is the *light* of my life.

Megan McKenzie (9)
St John the Baptist Primary School, Fauldhouse

Light

Light is the sun that creates shadows,
Light is my torch that helps me to see in the dark,
Light is the sun that rises in the morning,
Light is tinsel on my Christmas tree that shines in the morning,
Light is the sky that is bright in the daylight,
Light is my fireplace that is bright in the dark,
Light is the twinkling snow on Christmas Day,
Light is happiness,
Love is light.

Paul Lynch (9)
St John the Baptist Primary School, Fauldhouse

Light

Light is my torch guiding me to brightness,
Light is my lamp shining brightly around my room,
Light is the stars glowing brightly in the dark outside,
Light is the sun setting on the horizon,
Light is brightness to let me see,
Light is brightness to keep me safe,
Light is the sun that I see when I open my eyes,
Light is when my family is happy,
Light is a sign of love,
Light is the cars driving through the night,
A rainbow is light reflecting in the raindrops.

Jake Denholme (9)
St John the Baptist Primary School, Fauldhouse

Summer

Monday is a sunny day
And all the kids are out to play.

Tuesday we go down to the beach
And then we go to swim in the sea.

Wednesday is the time to play
And I play with my friends all day.

Thursday we go down to swim
And my trainer is called Tim.

Friday is the day to play,
Then we go out on our bikes.

Meghan Cairns (9)
St John the Baptist Primary School, Fauldhouse

Winter

I can feel the cold of the mist in the cold air,
You can't see the beautiful snow,
The little birds are singing of happiness,
You can touch and smell and feel the very cold air,
In sight of smell and touch and feel of the snow.

Thomas Warrington (10)
St John the Baptist Primary School, Fauldhouse

Summer Days

On Monday kids bought ice cream off the ice cream man,
On Tuesday we played outside in the boiling sun,
On Wednesday we went to the park and went sliding down the chute,
On Thursday we went to play with friends
And on Friday we did anything.

Taylor Lamont (9)
St John the Baptist Primary School, Fauldhouse

Summer Dreams

Monday was the best day, the sky would not turn to grey,
Tuesday night was very good but my mum was in a mood
And that was not good.
Wednesday morning was OK but at night I went away,
Thursday the sun shone bright, the same happened at night,
Friday was very sad, an old man tripped that very day,
But he was certainly OK.

Bryss Aitchison (9)
St John the Baptist Primary School, Fauldhouse

The Light

Light is the moon reflecting the sun,
Light is the torch that dances on the wall,
Light is my lamp protecting me from the dark,
Light is the sun shining through the window,
Light is the mirror reflecting the sunlight,
Light is a warm fire on a cold wintry night,
Light is the sun shining on raindrops and creating a rainbow,
Light is when the teacher says no homework,
Light is happiness,
Light is when the bell rings for home time,
Life is light.

Jamie Walker (9)
St John the Baptist Primary School, Fauldhouse

Light

Light is the reflection of the setting sun over the sea,
Light is a torch light dancing on the wall,
Light helps me to see when I can't,
Light is the moon shining brightly in the night sky,
Light is the headlamps guiding a car down a dark road,
A rainbow is a beam of light going through raindrops,
Happiness is light.

Michael Cairney (9)
St John the Baptist Primary School, Fauldhouse

Light

Light is the sun reflecting through the window on my face,
Light is the happiness of my life,
Light is the gateway to Heaven,
Light is a big ball of fire,
Light is the happiness of a child's first Holy Communion
When God shines upon them,
Light is a beautiful rainbow in the summer sky,
Light is a gateway that never ends,
Light is the happiness of my mum's newborn baby,
Happiness is light.

Lesleyanne Nimmo (9)
St John the Baptist Primary School, Fauldhouse

Light

Light comes from lots of different species,
Light is good fun,
Light is the sun shining on the bright day,
Light is the stars twinkling in the night sky,
Light is the laser torch that shines on my walls,
Light is the happiness of my family,
Light is a bright new day,
Life is light.

Taylor John Ball (9)
St John the Baptist Primary School, Fauldhouse

Light

Light is the sun shining brightly through the window,
Light is a glowing fire when it is dark,
Light is the Christmas tree lights that sparkle through the night,
Light is a torch that always dances on the wall,
Light helps us to see when it is dark,
Light is the lava in my lamp that makes lovely shapes,
Light is the stars twinkling brightly up in the dark blue sky,
Light makes me really happy in the morning,
Light is the reflection of the sun setting,
Light is when the teacher says no homework,
Light is a colourful rainbow that makes a
Reflection that shines on the ground,
Light is the sun setting in the west,
Happiness is light when I'm with my family,
Love is light.

Caitlin Hilson (9)
St John the Baptist Primary School, Fauldhouse

Light

Light is the sun shining through a transparent window,
Light is the hero saving me from my bad dreams,
Light is the glowing twinkle of snow,
Light is a family gathering for a wedding,
Light is a sparkle of my Christmas tree lights,
Light is the guide of my future,
Light is the saviour of the darkness,
Light is a glow stick flickering in a concert,
Light is a lovely sunset picnic.
Love is light!

Amy Ramsay (9)
St John the Baptist Primary School, Fauldhouse

Light

Light is the love of a couple,
Light is the lava in my lamp making bubbly shapes,
Light is the love on a Christmas Day,
Light is the sign of love,
Light is when your family get together,
Light is the sign of a new life,
Light is a bright star twinkling in the night.

Kayleigh Reid (9)
St John the Baptist Primary School, Fauldhouse

Light

Light is my Playboy lava lamp that sparkles through the night,
Light is a torch that dances on the wall in a spooky room,
Light is the sun of the starry sky above,
Light is when I'm with my family out at the weekend,
Light is, the bright sky in the lovely morning,
Light is the rainbow that the sun shines on the raindrops,
Light is when the teacher says no homework,
Light is the sun reflecting from the setting sun on the lovely beach,
Light is the sign of happiness,
Light is the sun setting in the west.
Light is the bright new day.

Teri Flannigan (9)
St John the Baptist Primary School, Fauldhouse

The Emotional Awards

Emotions are little furry things,
That turn up everywhere,
In the bathroom, on the sofa,
Even in your hair.

Happiness is a feeling that makes,
You whistle your cares away,
Confidence is a girl that always
Has a lot to say.

Impatience is a virtue that
Means you just can't wait,
Loathing is an adult who is
Stronger than just plain hate.

Jealousy is a green-eyed monster,
That doesn't have a mate,
Stress is an emotion that is often seen,
When you are late.

Now ladies and gentleman,
Please give a huge cheer,
For every emotion that got
An emotional award right
Here!

Sophie Halpin (11)
St John the Baptist Primary School, Fauldhouse

The Vengeance

James came to school today,
With a venomous glare,
Past the lines he strode,
With a lethal stare.

I looked at James with sympathy
And felt full of despair,
For the look upon his face,
That day would cut stone here and there.

He held a grudge on his best friend Gary,
So whenever Gary passed, he was spitefully named,
The look upon his face that day,
Suggested Gary would be maimed.

That afternoon during prayers,
James was full of impatience,
It would take more than their strong friendship,
To conclude their vengeance.

Sean McAnna (11)
St John the Baptist Primary School, Fauldhouse

Singing

Singing out loud and clear,
How many voices can you hear?
Let the amazing feeling flow,
Now let your fantastic voices glow!

How many notes can you see?
On the page sing with me,
I feel different every line,
Every emotion takes its time!

Some people scream and shout,
But that's not what singing's all about,
Every little tiny sound,
Seems to echo round and round!

Amy Hunter (11)
St John the Baptist Primary School, Fauldhouse

Sweet Revenge

Revenge,
Sometimes it can be sweet,
But it can be nasty,
Angry and annoyed much later,
Hateful.

Hateful,
Sometimes angry,
Sometimes it makes you cry,
Sometimes it makes you confused,
Empty.

Steven O'Mullan (12)
St John the Baptist Primary School, Fauldhouse

The Emotions Of My Heart

The love and happiness in my heart
Will never ever break apart,
It is always there and will never go,
I just wanted to tell you so.

There's also anger, there's also hate,
In my heart and in my mate,
Deep in my heart, I will find,
All the emotions once combined.

The emotions in my heart will never leave,
No matter how hard I try to believe,
They will always shine on to make me feel strong,
No matter if I'm right or wrong.

There may be some sadness,
There may be some sorrow,
Maybe today or maybe tomorrow,
This emotion will always be there,
In my heart even if I don't care.

Demi Malloy (11)
St John the Baptist Primary School, Fauldhouse

Puppy Love

My dogs,
I love my dogs, I think they're cute and vicious,
I saw my dogs in the window and knew they were the ones.

I play with them every day,
I like being around them,
They give me joy, they give me fun, I just love them.

They comfort me when I'm sad,
That's my dogs for you
And that's that.

Dylan Watson (11)
St John the Baptist Primary School, Fauldhouse

My Best Night

On a Monday night when doing FHE,
A big surprise awaited me,
Before it I was bored so bad,
When it came, I would never be sad.

When I saw it, I jumped with glee,
'It's the Nintendo wii'
At the sight,
I wanted to play all night.

James Mateer (11)
St John the Baptist Primary School, Fauldhouse

Cinquain Poem

Oh-oh,
My sore head hurts,
I don't feel very good,
I feel like going home right now,
Ow, ow.

Connor Morton
St John the Baptist Primary School, Fauldhouse

Cinquain Poems

Pet emotions

Pet store
A cute rabbit
I thought it was so cute
I loved it to bits, I named it . . .
Charlie.

So fun
I played with him
I loved the cute bunny
Cleaning his hutch is so smelly!
Bunny.

Birthday
I am now nine
I get a new bunny
He is very athletic now
Thumper.

Happy
I cuddled him
I cared for him always
I do still love the both of them
Rabbits.

Aaron Jack (11)
St John the Baptist Primary School, Fauldhouse

Love

Love could be anything,
Something that you care,
Your family, your pet, even your hair.

Love is always there,
It goes on forever,
The hearts can be broken,
But the love is there forever.

Love is there for everyone,
Even young and old,
Love is there for everyone,
Though sometimes it is cold.

Love is an emotion,
That is spread around the world,
Anyone can use it as it
Never becomes old.

Chloe Findlay (11)
St John the Baptist Primary School, Fauldhouse

Emotions

I cried with fear,
Just with a little tear,
It wasn't even scary,
It was just a little fairy.

Your love,
Sends me to the clouds above.

Having light,
Is a good sight,
It makes you happy,
As well as snappy.

Sean Timmins (12)
St John the Baptist Primary School, Fauldhouse

My Emotions

Emotions are things that pop up,
Wherever you go,
They pop up to and fro,
Some are sad, some are mad,
But emotions are emotions
And they're here to stay.

Andrew Hutchison (11)
St John the Baptist Primary School, Fauldhouse

Animal Love - Cinquains

One day
I got a pet
It was a black puppy
It was puppy love at first sight
It's true.

One night
My dad came home
He brought me a present
It was a very small goldfish
He swims.

One day
My mum came home
She brought me a small cat
It is called Snowflake, the small cat,
It purrs.

Erin Muirhead (11)
St John the Baptist Primary School, Fauldhouse

Emotions

Having light
Is a great sight
For me and you

Having sight
Is like having light
And my love is great with you.

David Dalziel (11)
St John the Baptist Primary School, Fauldhouse

My Emotions - Cinquains

Love
Love hearts,
Love is joyful
Love hearts are in the air
Love hearts scattered everywhere
Be loved.

Joy
Joyful
Joyful pleasure
Peace and joy at Christmas
Be joyful and be delightful
Pleasure.

Fear
Fearful
Fear and distress
Grizzly bears are fearsome
Anxiety is caused by fear
Fearsome.

Robyn Ovens (11)
St John the Baptist Primary School, Fauldhouse

Winter

Look!
What can you see?
The happy children
Making snowmen,
Just like me.

Listen!
What can you hear?
The people singing
Carols far or near.

Touch!
What can you feel?
The snowy snowflakes,
Falling in the field.

Sniff?
What can you smell?
The fresh wind outside that is ready to tell.

Iqra Ramzan (9)
St John the Baptist Primary School, Fauldhouse

Green Spring

Spring is getting greener,
The air is getting hot,
Spring is growing flowers,
My garden is getting nicer,
My life is getting lighter.

All animals are breeding now,
Lambs, horses, rabbits and foxes,
All the Earth is getting warm,
Heating goes off at night,
My life is fun,
It's getting warm.

Maree Rooney (10)
St John the Baptist Primary School, Fauldhouse

Winter

Monday is very tiring and the snow is quite inspiring,
Tuesday is quite alright and it has been snowing heavily all night,
Wednesday is my rest day, I am allowed to have fun
And go out to play,
Thursday is my training day, I can't go to training
Because the snow is deep today,
Friday is a half day and luckily it has not been snowing today.

Johnnie Sommerville (9)
St John the Baptist Primary School, Fauldhouse

Summer

Look

People tanning at the pool
Men playing lots of pool.

Look

Dad going naff
We are having a great laugh.

Look

I am having lots of fun
All in the sun.

Cameron Bennett (9)
St John the Baptist Primary School, Fauldhouse

The Bully/Victim

I used to be a bully as mean as can be,
I used to take people's lunches and scoff them down me,
I used to take people's money so they didn't have a bus fee,
I am a victim now because I have stopped
And now I feel the pain that I used to be,
There is a new bully in the school, as mean as can be
And I am the victim as helpless as can be.

Michelangelo Mario Antonio Mulholland (10)
St Peter's Primary School, Edinburgh

I Do Not Want To Go Back To School Ever Again

The bully at our school is so tall that he looks 7 foot to me,
My temper gets so high, I feel like punching him,
So he never comes to school again,
Because he thinks he is so smart,
He also takes my friends away from me,
One day he got all his friends to come and batter me up,
So they kicked me and punched me and locked me in a cupboard,
It was so dark, I wanted to hug my mum so tight
But I cannot see her glowing bright,
When I went home, I said to my mum,
'I do not want to go to school ever again.'

Kieran Watt (10)
St Peter's Primary School, Edinburgh

If I Was A Bully

If I was a bully I would steal your lunch money
And kick you and run away.

If I was a bully I would pull your hair and
I would push you in a muddy puddle.

If I was a bully I would punch you
In the nose and kick you.

If I was a bully I would hide all your things
And run away with them.

If I was a bully I would talk behind your back.

If I was a bully I would hurt you and spy on you all the time.

But that's not true, I'm not a bully, I'm just like you.

Glen Paterson (9)
St Peter's Primary School, Edinburgh

If I Were A Bully

If I were a bully I would kick your hand,
Push you over so you don't stand.

If I were a bully I would go on a boat to the sea,
Guess who is driving, it's not me.

If I were a bully what would I do?
Steal your jotter, hide your shoe.

If I were a bully I would shave and pull your hair.

If I were a bully I would kick a ball and not share,
It would not be fair.

If I were a bully, what would I do?
Kick some dirt right at you.

If I were a bully, what would I do?
Steal a bike, even a shoe.

If I were a bully I would kick and hurt and push you in dirt.

So bullying is not fair,
Standing on your shoe, pulling your hair,
So stop bullying, it is not fair.

Josh Proctor (9)
St Peter's Primary School, Edinburgh

If I Were A Bully

If I were a bully,
I would punch your nose.
If I were a bully,
I would take your lunch,
If I were a bully,
Would you be my friend?
If I were a bully,
Would you share your
Sweets and toys,
If I were a bully,
I would chuck you on a hedge,
If I were a bully,
I would go canoeing with you rowing,
Thank goodness I'm not a bully,
I'm just like you.

Nathan Speedman (9)
St Peter's Primary School, Edinburgh

My Pet Rat

Two shining black eyes as dark as the night sky,
Peering curiously around.

Two bat-like ears standing proud and alert, always on patrol.

A cute, snuffly sniffer constantly seeking odours
Surrounded by ever-twitching whiskers.

With long orange blades in her food-seeking mouth,
She grinds and crunches and gnaws her food.

A grey stripe on her back leads down to her long tail
Which gropes around helping her balance like a
Tightrope walker.

She never fails to delight.
My rat Mic.

Christopher Turnbull (10)
St Peter's Primary School, Edinburgh

There's A Bully In Our School

There's a bully in our school,
She picks on me because I am small,
She takes my lunch money,
She steals my stuff.

She looks at my answers,
When I'm not looking,
She kicks me under the table,
She won't let me join in games,
She tricks me, then gets me into trouble.

She steals my pencil and
Then won't give it back,
She trips me up in the playground
And then makes me hurt myself,
By pushing me over.

She takes away my friends
When I'm playing with them,
She can hurt my feelings by calling me names,
I feel very sad and upset on the outside,
But I feel cold and empty on the inside.

I want to tell the teacher but if I do,
She'll do more bad things to me,
But finally I went up to the teacher quietly
And told her what she was doing to me,
She got in trouble, I am not a bully,
I am a normal person just like you.

Theresa Wong (9)
St Peter's Primary School, Edinburgh

Why?

Why do they stop and stare?
Why do they always glare?
Why are they always there?
Oh why, why, why?

Why do they pick on me?
Why do they beat me up?
Why do they not like me?
Oh why, why, why?

Why do they call me names?
Why do they tease me?
Why can't I play their games?
Oh why, why, why?

Is it because I am different
And eat lots of different things?
Is it because my skin is black?
Oh why, why, why?

Anna Service (10)
St Peter's Primary School, Edinburgh

I Am Scared!

When I run down the corridors, I am scared,
When I am doing my work, I am scared,
When I am in the playground, I am scared,
When I am going to school, I am scared,
When I walk home, I am scared,
When I am anywhere, I am scared . . .
Because the bullies are out to get me . . .
Well that's what they say
And I am getting scared,
More and more each day.

Sally Cairns (10)
St Peter's Primary School, Edinburgh

The Bullies

I go round the corner and there they are,
Standing around or sitting on a car,
'Hello David,' one of them says with a leer,
The others all laugh and smirk and sneer,
'Give us the money,' says another one,
'OK,' I say, I want to run,
But I can't, my legs are as stiff as wood,
I wouldn't have fought back, even if I could,
They're strong and brave and they have no fears,
I'm just a coward that sheds loads of tears,
I chuck the money into their hand,
Then one kicks me and it hurts when I land,
I pick myself up about to walk away,
But I turn round this time, I feel different today,
'Give me my money, give it back right now,'
They drop it and run, I did it, I just don't know how,
I pick up the money from the grubby street,
I'm pleased with myself because the bullies are beat.

Jacob Kennedy (10)
St Peter's Primary School, Edinburgh

Bullying!

I'm walking along the railway track,
I see them coming, I run, run for my life,
I'm stuck, I have nowhere to go,
They catch me,
They take my T-shirt,
They pull me against the wall,
They criticise me, beat me up,
I fall, they go, I run,
Suddenly I can see a way,
I run to my freedom but
Without a catch of breath the door closes,
I search, I can't hear anything,
I keep running, then I see another way out
Of the horrible life that I have,
Then I stop and fall to the ground
And stop breathing,
Suddenly I die!

James Flynn (10)
St Peter's Primary School, Edinburgh

Racism Poem

Racism is an offence and horrid,
Nobody likes it so what's the point,
Every day I get abuse - why?
That's up to the racists but I don't know why.

Come on racists, don't do it,
That's why I don't like abuse,
Racists said it's fun but I can't see how,
Why are they doing this? But at the end of the day,
They only have themselves to blame.

Come on racists please don't do this,
I don't like it,
Why should I get abuse?
Is it the way I look?
But that's just me.

Michael Monan (10)
St Peter's Primary School, Edinburgh

Why Does It Happen To Me, Why Me?

Back to school after the weekend,
I feel my life is coming to an end,
Because of the bullies that kick and punch me,
Why does it happen to me, why me?

After school they chase me home,
They are so mean, never leave me alone,
They chase me, tease me, kick and punch me,
Why does it happen to me, why me?

When I first got bullied I was six years old,
It stopped for a year, then I was told,
'Give me your money or I'll beat you up,'
Why does it happen to me, why me?

It happens a lot, every single day,
I wish for once, that they would pay,
I hate them, they hate me, I hate them more,
Why does it happen to me, why me?

I want it to end, end right now,
They call me names like Pooh and Cow,
My life is a misery, how shall I tell?
Why does it happen to me, *why me?*

Molly Donovan (10)
St Peter's Primary School, Edinburgh

To A Bully

How evil is the bully who bugs me every day?
How evil is the bully who hurts me all the time?
The bully, my most feared fear of all,
How much I hate the bully who always plays the fool,
How much I hate the bully who never gives in at all,
How may I beat the bully my most feared fear of all?

Peter Rennie (10)
St Peter's Primary School, Edinburgh

Just Because I'm Different . . .

In the morning I'm scared to go to school,
For when I get there, I feel like a fool,
It doesn't feel right,
When they push me around,
Just because I'm different.

When I'm in the playground,
They punch me to the ground
And when I go to the locker room,
They whack me with a broom,
Just because I'm different.

Every single day they hurt me,
It feels like I'm being plonked in the sea,
Swooshed away by the black current,
Into a horrible darkness,
Just because I'm different.

After a while they left me alone,
They learnt I wasn't made of stone,
I felt bigger and stronger
And never left out,
I'm no longer different.

Emily McHugh (10)
St Peter's Primary School, Edinburgh

Why Me?

Why do you pick on me?
I can't get home in time for tea,
Because you would not let me go,
A smile my family will not see me show.

I scream as I arrive at school
And you push me into the pool,
Now I am freezing wet,
Anything you do to me, you will regret.

I'm not strong, actually quite weak,
Then I hear the door creak,
I'm scared, I don't know what to do,
Well, not pant like a kangaroo.

But now we're friends,
Sometimes the metal bends,
But never breaks,
It feels like I'm eating a lot of cakes.

Charlotte McGowan (10)
St Peter's Primary School, Edinburgh

Running

I'm running,
Running away from them,
They're laughing, screaming, shouting,
I can't bear to listen to them.

I won't stop running,
Not until I'm as far away from them,
I have found a cupboard,
I lock myself into it,
Never to return to that horrible world again.

The door is rattling,
Someone is there,
The door is flung, they're standing in front of me,
Glaring.

Kieran Fitzgerald (10)
St Peter's Primary School, Edinburgh

Bullying

B ullying is very nasty,
U s victims don't like it at all,
L ately it's got extremely bad,
L ike a cough turned into a cold,
Y ou really don't want to bully,
I t's not nice and you know it too,
N ow listen well to me bullies,
G o and change your nasty habits.

Daniel Pacitti (10)
St Peter's Primary School, Edinburgh

Why?

Why is it always me?
Why do I get punched?
Why am I sad?
Why have I got a broken arm?

Why is it frightening?
Why am I cold?
Why am I so lonely?
Why doesn't the teacher know?

Why is the bully bad?
Why am I scared?
Why can't I just run away?
Why won't I be left alone?

Gilian Reid (10)
St Peter's Primary School, Edinburgh

The Racist

I saw it all yesterday,
The poor girl was struck down,
Just because she was black,
He thought she was a clown.

He teased her all day,
It made her upset,
Because she is scared,
She's not told anyone yet.

She's run away now,
I'm glad about that,
The racist then followed,
But tripped over a cat.

He got back up,
Started chasing again,
But the girl turned around,
She'd reached her friend Ben.

She said to the racist,
'Go away now!'
Ben added in,
'We cannot allow!'

The racist was shocked
And he ran away,
The girl was then happy,
That she could now play.

Tom Jarvis (10)
St Peter's Primary School, Edinburgh

Trapped

I'm in a dark corner,
With no way out,
I shut my eyes and the walls come closer,
Why me? A voice says inside
And all my courage goes aside.

There's kicking and shoving
And no one seems to be loving,
My friends are gone,
But I still need to be *strong*,
I think I'm going to cry,
Although they just want me to die!

I wish I knew why,
Why they will not hear my cry,
I try to sneak away,
But there is nowhere I can play.

Each dead end leads to another
And I wish I could reach out and hug my mother,
But this is their way,
The way to gruesomely play.

These people are called bullies,
But they're worse than a bull,
They make me want to jump,
Jump down, down to the deepest point,
Where no one else will go.

Rian McDermott (10)
St Peter's Primary School, Edinburgh

Recipe For No Bullying

A pinch of happiness,
A teaspoon of hope.

A cup of courage,
A spoonful of love.

A hint of kindness,
A handful of life and welcome.

And into the oven of justice,
Wait for 13 believing minutes.

And enjoy a non-bullying surprise.

Daniella McGinley (9)
St Peter's Primary School, Edinburgh

Dreaming You're A Bully

I have a best friend,
She's started playing with these other people,
They're the bullies of the school.

I've told her all my
Deepest, darkest secrets,
I can't do anything about it,
Or she'll stomp her big feet all over me.

Sitting by myself in the toilets,
No one came to see me,
It felt like a flight of stairs that never ends.

I am a frightened goldfish
And I am scared to be eaten,
Up by a black cat.

I feel the pain in my heart,
Nobody's asked if I'm OK,
I am a lion in a cage,
Not able to break free.

But then I wake up
And my best friend is there,
Sitting by my side,
With a plate of
Chocolate biscuits!

Ellen McGrath (9)
St Peter's Primary School, Edinburgh

The Seaside

The sea roars,
The children play,
People swimming on a hot sunny day,
People sailing, fish in the sea,
Some people fishing with bait made of clay,
Some people throwing frisbees very high,
The dogs and cats jumping around,
Trying to dig up a bone they found,
Scientists digging for fossils and jewels,
Some people playing in the hotel pools.

Matthew Messer (9)
St Peter's Primary School, Edinburgh

There's A Bully In Our School

There's a bully in our school,
There's a selfish bully in our school,
When I see him bullying someone I fill up with hatred,
There's a selfish, angry bully in our school,
Now I know bullying's mean and wrong, but did you know?
He's only selfish, angry, mean and also a coward.

Patrick Mulvanny (9)
St Peter's Primary School, Edinburgh

If I Were A Bully

If I were a bully I would swipe your ball,
If I were a bully I would call you small.

If I were a bully I would steal your lunch,
If I were a bully I would give your nose a punch.

If I were a bully I would rip your work,
If I were a bully I would steal your shoe.

If I were a bully I would copy your answers,
If I were a bully would call you Prancer.

If I were a bully I would pull your hair,
But I am not a bully and that's fair!

Kirsty Anderson (9)
St Peter's Primary School, Edinburgh

If I Were A Bully

If I were a bully, I would
Punch and kick you,
If I were a bully, I would
Shove you downstairs,
If I were a bully, I would
Make you do my homework,
If I were a bully, I would
Steal your answers,
If I were a bully I would
Talk behind your back,
If I were a bully, I would
Make you bleed,
If I were a bully, I would
Steal your bike,
If I were a bully, I would
Be racist,
If I were a bully, I would
Be nasty,
If I were a bully, I would
Tease you.

If I were a bully,
But this is not true,
I am not a bully,
Just like you.

Jack Crookston (10)
St Peter's Primary School, Edinburgh

If I Were A Bully

If I were a bully I would
Steal your toys.

If I were a bully I would
Kick you until you cry.

If I were a bully I would
Make you do my homework.

If I were a bully I would
Steal your lunch money.

If I were a bully I would
Break your arm.

If I were a bully I would
Throw you at a spiky fence.

If I were a bully I would
Make you row my canoe.

But I'm not a bully,
I'm an ordinary boy just like you.

John Dunn-Butler (9)
St Peter's Primary School, Edinburgh

Katie And Her Big Boots

Katie came stomping up to me with her big boots,
All the noise of the playground,
Became silence in my ears,
Just the noise of her boots,
Stomp! Stomp! Stomp!

I felt fear,
Starting to creep into me,
She saw my eyes
And came towards me.

I turned around,
As her boots hit my shins,
I fell to the ground,
I heard and saw,
The flash of mobile phones and the click of videos.

The humiliation that I'd felt so often,
Came back into my body again,
Then warm happiness,
Beat the humiliation,
A P7 came and picked me up
And sat me down
And started to shout at Katie.

I felt something that day,
That I'd never felt before,
Happiness,
A P7 and me had beaten Katie with her big boots.

Louise Goode (9)
St Peter's Primary School, Edinburgh

If I Were A Bully

If I were a bully,
I'd make you do what I say,
I'd be horrible to you,
I'd not let you play.

If I were a bully,
I'd push you in the air,
I'd take your lunch money,
I'd pull your hair.

If I were a bully,
I'd push you around,
I'd make you cry,
I'd make you kneel on the ground.

If I were a bully,
I'd pinch you and poke you,
I'd hide all your things,
I'd not let you do what you wanted to do.

But I'm not a bully
And I'm glad,
Because if I was,
I'd be sad!

Amanda Kostryckyj (9)
St Peter's Primary School, Edinburgh

If I Were A Bully

If I were a bully I would laugh at your face.
If I were a bully I would pull your hair.
If I were a bully I would steal your ball.

If I were a bully I would squeeze your nose.
If I were a bully I would steal your money.
If I were a bully I would pull your ears.

If I were a bully I would be violent to you.
If I were a bully I would push you.
If I were a bully I would trick you.

If I were a bully I would put a needle on your chair.
If I were a bully I would call you fatty.

But I'm not a bully really.

Gianluca Cuthbertson (9)
St Peter's Primary School, Edinburgh

The Tiny Boy

The tiny boy,
Is poor as poor,
Strong as buffaloes,
Massive socks,
Too big for him,
Blond hair,
Frighteningly frizzy,
With a wound,
So painful,
Limping around.

The tiny boy,
So alarmed, scared, lonely,
No friends and
Neglected like
A wild animal,
He lost his family,
In the scary streets.

The tiny boy,
Looking desperately,
For his family,
Under the rubble,
Very hungry, but
Will dig until
He finds them.

Kirsty Summers (9)
Wardie Primary School, Edinburgh

Your Turn

I stood there with my tufty hair
And watched the other children stare,
The same words going round my head,
The words my mother said,
I saw the man on the other side,
Walking straight and full of pride,
He knelt down by a child's side and said,
'Your turn.'

My body filled with lumps of fright,
I sat and watched that awful sight,
As scared as a little tiny mouse,
I sat outside that murder house,
I saw the man on the other side,
Walking straight and full of pride,
He knelt down by a child's side and said,
'Your turn.'

I wait here in the giant line,
Waiting, waiting for my time,
There are no smiles in this camp
Inside here it's cold and damp
I see the man from the other side
Walking straight and full of pride,
He kneels down by my side and says,
'Your turn.'

Hayley Scott (9)
Wardie Primary School, Edinburgh

In London There Is A Boy

In London there is a boy,
Lonely and sad,
Nobody to talk to,
Help him look for food,
Everybody laughing at him.

In London there is a boy,
Who is dirty,
Heartbroken and alone,
No family,
Mum or dad, granny or grandad.

In London there is a boy,
In a bomb suit,
As brave as a tiger,
Hiding from the army,
He must find the courage to go.

Aaron Heinemeier (9)
Wardie Primary School, Edinburgh

Blue Sights - Haiku

Blue sights splash on rocks
With reflections on the sea
The sky is blue too.

Louis Malcolm (9)
Wardie Primary School, Edinburgh

Walking In Sadness

Alone,
Cheeks flushed with sorrow,
Salty tears dripping, dripping,
Sad songs of solitude,
Eyes shining like bowls full of sapphires,
Brimming over with loneliness.

Alone,
He sobbed,
In the bleak, barren rubble,
Distraught,
Seeking but a word of comfort,
A hand extended in friendship.

Alone,
His parents dead,
Protectors gone,
Abandoned and terrified,
Alone for life,
Because of the bomb.

Freya Dixon-van Dijk (9)
Wardie Primary School, Edinburgh

The Sad Boy

The boy looks sad,
Upset and unhappy,
Crying,
Worried,
Poor,
He looks scared,
Gloomy,
Disappointed,
Tearful.

The boy looks sad,
Sorrowful and scared,
Troubled,
Depressed,
Tearful,
He looks as scared as a mouse,
Running
Away
From
A cat.

Nancy Brown (9)
Wardie Primary School, Edinburgh

The Stone

As rough as sandpaper,
As sparkly as the sea,
The stone is glinting and glistening,
Glittery and grey,
Silvery and shiny,
Sparkly and speckled,
Smooth,
Round,
Rough,
Stone.

Matthew Fischbacher (9)
Wardie Primary School, Edinburgh

The Stone

The rough, swirly, black waters,
Smoothly,
Shape the shiny stone,
Like sandpaper,
Smoothly,
Shapes wood.

Marcus Chapman (9)
Wardie Primary School, Edinburgh

Summer

The sun has come back to us,
The grass is green and perfect length,
The trees are big and bushy,
The children are busy playing in the park,
Smokey BBQs in gardens,
Huge mountains shining in the sun,
Happy people smiling on the street,
Ice creams dripping along the beach,
The flowers are out and the colours are bright
And the temperature is rising in our houses.

Cameron Soutar (9)
Wormit Primary School, Wormit

Just About Spring

Blood-red crabapples blazing in the sun,
The wind is still blowing in the treetops,
The leaves have all trickled down
And others have just begun to grow,
The snow is starting to fade away
And the sun is coming out,
The birds are now singing and
Children playing,
In the cold spring park.

John Nelson (10)
Wormit Primary School, Wormit

I Can't Stop Shopping

I can't stop shopping,
I shop in loads of shops,
I look at lovely sparkly shoes
And drool over frilly tops,
Floral dresses catch my eye
And so do teeny-weenie mini skirts,
Round flash earrings,
Big silver bracelets in the light,
I love to shop,
But my mum says to stop,
I try to stop, honest I do.

Megan Dempster (10)
Wormit Primary School, Wormit

Snow Is Here

The snow is sprinkling down to the ground,
Innocent wrapped up children are having fun,
But soon the blizzards are blowing hard,
Lakes are frozen,
The trees are crusted with the frost,
Breath freezes in the air,
Your fingers go white and numb.

Alexander Rowan (9)
Wormit Primary School, Wormit

My Dragon

My dragon is called Joy,
She's one of my best friends,
She walks to school and back with me,
The fun never ends,
We went to the park one day,
But nobody else was there,
So we had our own little party,
Then all my friends came.
Joy toasted the marshmallows with her breath
And I made the tea and we played tig,
But beware not all dragons are alike,
Some are much more fierce,
But my Joy is a little pet.

Rebecca Weir (9)
Wormit Primary School, Wormit

The Winds Of The Winter

The winds of the winter,
Bitter and cold,
Snow fills the streets,
The clouds go grey with the cold
An old man with his hat fights the wind to his car,
Water turns to ice,
A child slips and cries for help,
Her mother picks her loved child up,
Then battles the bitter wind home,
Soon the town will be in darkness,
As the snowflakes fall.

Susannah Rosemary McWhirter (9)
Wormit Primary School, Wormit

Spring Has Come

Lambs and foals and kids and calves,
They all play in fields of grass,
Winter's done,
Spring has come,
Look at all the flowers.

Foals are brown, lambs are white,
Light breezes blowing, sun shining bright,
Winter's done,
Spring has come,
Chasing winter away.

Under the bright yellow sun,
Where children have fun,
Winter's done,
Spring has come
And so has the shining sun.

Big trees swaying in the gentle breeze,
Foals still lying on their knees,
Winter's done,
Spring has come,
Just look outside and see.

Freya Simpson (9)
Wormit Primary School, Wormit

The Spring Fairy

The spring fairy travels on the light breeze,
She collects the last winter berries,
Shining red and delicious they taste.

She dances off the buds of green daffodils,
Tickles the top of lambs' noses,
Skips across fields smelling the long sweet grass,
Sunlight glinting over the hill.

If you blink, you will miss her!

Eve Gourlay (9)
Wormit Primary School, Wormit

Lonely Night

Lonely as a wolf crying to the moon,
How alone, how lonely.

Lonely is the sun when its face is hidden
By the black-hearted clouds,
How sad, how lonely.

Lonely is the tree, his neighbours have
Been cut down, how lonely.

Spring is here, winter is gone,
Mates for forlorn wolves, not alone!

Spring is here, winter is gone,
The sun shows his face, not sad.

Spring is here, winter is gone,
Trees are starting to grow,
Not lonely.

But away winter goes, how lonely.

Clodagh Ryan (9)
Wormit Primary School, Wormit

The Sea Monster

A ferocious creature living in the depths of the deep blue sea,
A monster with scaly skin and disgusting breath,
Sharp, pointy teeth with blood-red eyes
And claws like razor blades,
It eats sailors sailing across the big deep sea,
No one hears their screams,
None of them come home.

Robin Black (10)
Wormit Primary School, Wormit

Cowboys

Cowboys riding in the glistening sun,
Reflecting off their gold skin,
Rampaging around,
The ground is shaking,
The golden sand is sizzling,
The sun
Goes down, disappearing into the
Horizon,
The cowboys make camp,
Soon the fire is blazing red-hot,
One
By one they curl up to sleep,
Around
The fire.

Adam Nish (9)
Wormit Primary School, Wormit

Friends Poem

Friends tell you secrets,
Friends always play,
Friends send you postcards when they go away,
Friends help you out when you are down,
Friends help you tidy up,
Friends help you out when you are hurt,
Friends are always there.

Anne-Marie Marshall (9)
Wormit Primary School, Wormit

The Spring Breezes

Hear the robins singing in the trees,
See the leaves fluttering in the breeze,
The shining sun is warming the ground,
Little lambs bounding round and round.

Little green buds of daffodils just beginning to grow,
Tiny white snowdrops nodding their heads,
The buds on the trees turning green,
The last of the autumn leaves still lie on the ground.

Eleanor Heighton (9)
Wormit Primary School, Wormit

Just About Spring

Bright sunshine warms the ground,
Blood-red crab apples hanging on the trees,
Bleating lambs that have lost their mum searching in the mild sun,
Noisy crows cawing in the breeze,
Breadcrumbs ready to be eaten thrown by the farmer's wife
As she gazes at the beautiful sunshine.
Blackbirds singing nearby,
The world is coming back to life,
Here comes spring!

Phoebe Martin (9)
Wormit Primary School, Wormit

Where Teachers Rule The School

It's not that easy to survive,
In a school that's got an army of teachers,
They hunt you down wielding rulers,
Once you step inside their lounge (aka: torture chamber),
You don't go back for tea,
The janitor is also a gangster,
Patrolling the streets with a mop,
Here are some of the teachers' favourite books,
'The Beauty of Rulers',
'How to rip children's hair out'
And 'Cooking Children',
Don't play with globes,
Because the geography teachers put them on self-destruct,
There's no playtime or lunch,
If you're out of line,
It's the cleaner's closet for you,
The maths books are on paper-cut mode,
You'd be lucky to get homework,
Because not too many go home
And if you try to escape,
Just don't do it mate!

Rory Strathie (9)
Wormit Primary School, Wormit

Young Writers Information

We hope you have enjoyed reading this book - and that you will continue to enjoy it in the coming years.

If you like reading and writing poetry drop us a line, or give us a call, and we'll send you a free information pack.

Alternatively if you would like to order further copies of this book or any of our other titles, then please give us a call or log onto our website at www.youngwriters.co.uk

**Young Writers Information
Remus House
Coltsfoot Drive
Peterborough
PE2 9JX**

(01733) 890066

**WRECKING BALL PRESS
HULL • ISSUE 5**

the reater

EDITOR & WHIP CRACKER

SHANE RHODES

Design & Cover Illustration   by   Owen Benwell

With special thanks to Claire Hutchings
& Fiona Arnott

©All Copyright remains with the artists & contributors.
Unless for the purposes of review or drunken recitation do not attempt to reproduce any part of this periodical.

This edition of the reater has been funded by the
Arts Council of England

**All submissions, subscriptions,
and any other material should be sent to :**
The Reater
9 Westgate
North Cave
Brough
East Yorkshire
HU15 2NG

Published in 2000 by Wrecking Ball Press

table of contents

rodney wood
- postcards from the hall, 1951 11
- first aider, the early days 12
- the swing of the floor polisher 13

peter ardern
- allman's farm 17
- sea-life 18

brian docherty
- manchesters big mistake 23
- showtime 24
- situational ethnicity for beginners 25
- Bernard's Bumper Joke Book, p.18 26

(picture by **dee rimbaud**)

sean burn
- jackson pollock 33
- sellin january 34
- 134, #2 35

virgil saurez
- postal 39
- las palomas voladoras, or how cubans came to know their bicycles 40
- when the great chinese papermakers came to cuba, the great poets followed 41
- bay of pigs revisited 42
- canticle of the breasts 43
- distopia, or bhaktin & derrida mud-wrestle for fun & profit 44

felicity tumpkin
- underneath 47

(picture by **dee rimbaud**)

steve timms
    compilation..50

steve sneyd
    needing Ancestral Help 52

jacqueline karp
    yves 53

james prue
    juggling on brighton beach 54

andrew parker
    underneath 55

mary rudbeck stanko
    zen dream...56

ken smith
    apples be damned..57

peter carpenter
    the royal scam 58

david roberts
    fisticuffs 59

david lyall
    april 1995, AD 60

jacqueline sousa
    door to door 61

jo pearson
    going to the bottle bank 62

brendan mcmahon
evening 63

(picture by **dee rimbaud**)

dave newman
gravity 69

(picture by **dee rimbaud**)

anna woodford
99% perspiration 89
evening class 90

finella davenport
skinheads, 1978 95
on skates 96

b. z. niditch
outside a paris cafe 101
odd city 102
impramatur 103

(picture by **dee rimbaud**)

robert nazarene
nutshell 109
at the pistol-whip bar & grill 110
treebonics 111
little mister 112

rosemary palmeira
the return 117
crossing the water 118

rodney wood
Farnborough, England

Postcards From The Hall, 1951

E NORWAY, SELECTING FROM THE VINTAGE
CELLARS

A lot of people don't make the connection
between a restaurant with a wine
list and this cellar probably because cellars
are supposed to be old and the restaurant's
not called something French like Le Gavroche.
Today's not a good one to have
my photo taken, to exhibit myself.
I was celebrating with the devil sperm
last night and my head's sore and my
saliva tastes like vinegar or the sediment
from beer casks. But I wouldn't have missed
that blur of lust and desire,
the quietness of when I was inside Paula
who's cheap, bubbly and goes down well.

FIRST AIDER, THE EARLY DAYS

I'm waiting for something like the Great
Boston Molasses Flood with a wall of
treacle 15 ft high killing people, horses
executed because they were trapped like flies.
My accident book is empty although
I expect my child sitter will have one
with her boyfriend. There's a bed
here, single mattress, three pillows – but that
gooseberry between my legs is forbidden fruit.
At work I'm known as Sister Iceberg,
wear a porkpie hat, my voice
echoes in the halls. But at home
I wonder what I'll be blamed for, am afraid
of his huge hands that've forgotten how to be tender.

THE SWING OF THE FLOOR POLISHER

It was taken on a Friday, pay
day, looks like I'm headed for an
important date, my ambition is to own
a car, be married six times. I've
no interest in Bach and classical stuff
but it's good here a new hall
unused floor, laminate not lino, that shines
up so easily with this four-wheel buffer.
I promised mother I'd wear this jumper
spilt some tea down it though, Ernest
said it looked like something else. At
night on my way home smoke from
the trains, bodies along the Embankment and me,
with a limp, looking for someone to love.

peter ardern
Hull, England

Allman's Farm

Somewhere in a sky-lit studio, in a converted barn in Sussex
Your demise has been plotted.
Medieval banners already proclaim total victory
All along the blackthorn hedge.

'Those who cut the red hawthorn tree
Will ever frail and cursed be....'

We used to think druids consorted in this grove...
No doubt soon the empire of Dimmock will swallow you up
The hoof-trodden hollow will become a black-lined idyll
Stickle-backs in the drain will give way to shabunkins

I can hear the clank of the rusty latch drop
I can see the ruddy hand scoop into the churn
I can taste yellow cream before it was sterilised
I can smell damson-blossom and damp hay and dung

No straight-edged mind could draft this place
Hard generations made this, time and chance
Edged by nature hardly kept at bay

You random gods of nook and cranny, where are you?
There is no Minister of Allman's Farm....
There is no lobbyist for magic.

Sea-life

Out of the cliffs at Whitby it came.
A fossil, a fish, forget the Latin name
Delivered by a bespectacled bit
Of newly-graduated stuff.

Every bone in the spine is visible
Each tiny fin pristine
Still pushing along
Still bog-eyed
Still the fish it was thirty million years ago.

Like all temporary life-forms
It thought it was eternal.
And here it is on my mantel-piece
Between a Hull Sharks mug
And a fishermans needle.

My son asks
"Do we all end up like that?"

"Not the likes of us son.
David Beckham, maybe....
Not the likes of us....."

brian docherty
London, England

Manchester's Big Mistake
(Brian Sewell, Evening Standard)

Is being Manchester. Too Irish, too Jewish,
too bloody Northern for Brian Sewell's taste.
We can't have a Holocaust Museum here
just because a few Asiatics escaped some
pogrom or other. Who remembers Armenia
in 1915 he drawls; we do Brian, we do.
We don't have the luxury of aestheticising
experience, of pretending only socially
conscious art is 'political', forgetting Wilde
wrote 'The Soul of Man under Socialism'.
Picasso's all right nailed to the Prado wall,
Brecht's all right entombed in the Olivier,
Irish music's all right cordoned off on Radio 2,
the history of Cottonopolis can accommodate
Hard Times or Engels without bothering too
much about the likes of Mary & Lizzie Burns
whose labour power produced the profits,
whose class consciousness educated Engels
whose money gave Marx leisure to do his work;
he should have a watchmaker or tailor,
kept his place & lost his dreams, both of them.
Manchester is full of people whose grandparents
found out too late that Salford was not Brooklyn,
and this would have to be home. Cheated?
Of course not; Manchester isn't England,
I mean it's not the Home Counties, Brian.
But if you ignore the weather & the food,
strange looking people with peculiar accents,
it's preferable to Vilna, Belfast or Armenia,
anywhere else people hate you for being different.

Showtime
(Richard Beamish, 1899-1977)

Great-Uncle Dick started as a clog dancer
learning his trade on a pub's cellar doors.
When he was 12 he refused Poplar's options,
auditioned for Sam Richards' Six White Boys,
made his debut at Camden's Bedford Theatre.

This subject of Sickert's *Noctes Ambrosianae*
was erased in 1968 by a Nationwide branch
but in 1911 clog dancing almost had a future.
In the 20s he joined J.W. Jackson's English Dancers
who stickered his suitcase with half of Europe.

In the 30s his matinee idol was Dick Powell.
West End managements gave him steady work
sharing dressing rooms with John McCormick
and a litany of names faded beyond sepia.
651 performances in *The White Horse Inn*.

He signed up with ENSA for War work then
soldiered on as Sergeant in 'The Raw Recruit'
in the 1946 Royal Variety Performance
After the music halls went dark in the 50s,
Dick never transferred to TV or radio.

He took one role in 'straight theatre' then,
his pal Larry asking "Dick d'you want a job?"
"What all that Shakespearian rubbish" his comeback,
Bottom at the Old Vic a treat for the family,
the best pantomime horse in the world ever.

In the 60s he could still dance a step or two
of the routines he toured with Gracie Fields
round theatres only property developers remember.
His legacy is a battered case of sheet music
thumbed to tatters by rehearsal pianists.

Situational Ethnicity For Beginners

After the Inverness Folk Festival
we camped at Castle Urquhart
drinking beer & telling Nessie jokes
till 2 am brought the Beastie herself
to scramble us into the car.
At lunchtime the locals in the
Drumnadrochit Hotel scowled
at long hair, guitars, requests
for Guinness & ashet pies.
laughing in Gaelic at rusty
splutters from the tap.
The barman dredged up enough
English to say *Sorry*, offering
a choice of 5 beers, 21 whiskies.
Grasping the familiar gleam
of Newkie Broon with relief
we outraged the teuchters
by singing *Death Of A Clown*.
We gave them every Bowie,
Lou Reed & Stones song we knew
till the landlord offered to
demonstrate his collection
of 'cultural weapons' demanding
to know were we Campbells.
We thanked him in Lallans
for this Highland hospitality.
bought 2 crates of Broon
for the drive to Fort William,
took his daughters & nieces with us.
Céad Míle Fáilte.

Bernard's Bumper Joke Book, p.18

These two feminists from Birmingham
Fatima & Leila decide to go on holiday.
"I fancy somewhere foreign" says Fatima
"Yeh something exotic how about Wales?"

So they're cycling through Shropshire
and it's getting towards lunchtime.
They don't like the look of the villages
the villages don't like the look of them.

Market Day in the next decent size town.
"There must be a veggie restaurant here."
When they marched into the Masonic Arms
a long roomful of farmers fell silent.

"Is it something I said or what?"
"Nah they just can't understand your accent."
So they take a table near the door.
"Check the graffiti – can't even spell PAKI."

Farmer Jones shoots past singing *Sospan Fach*.
Back of the Landrover his sons & two sheep.
"Look at that that's disgusting that is."
"I know I really hate them arranged marriages."

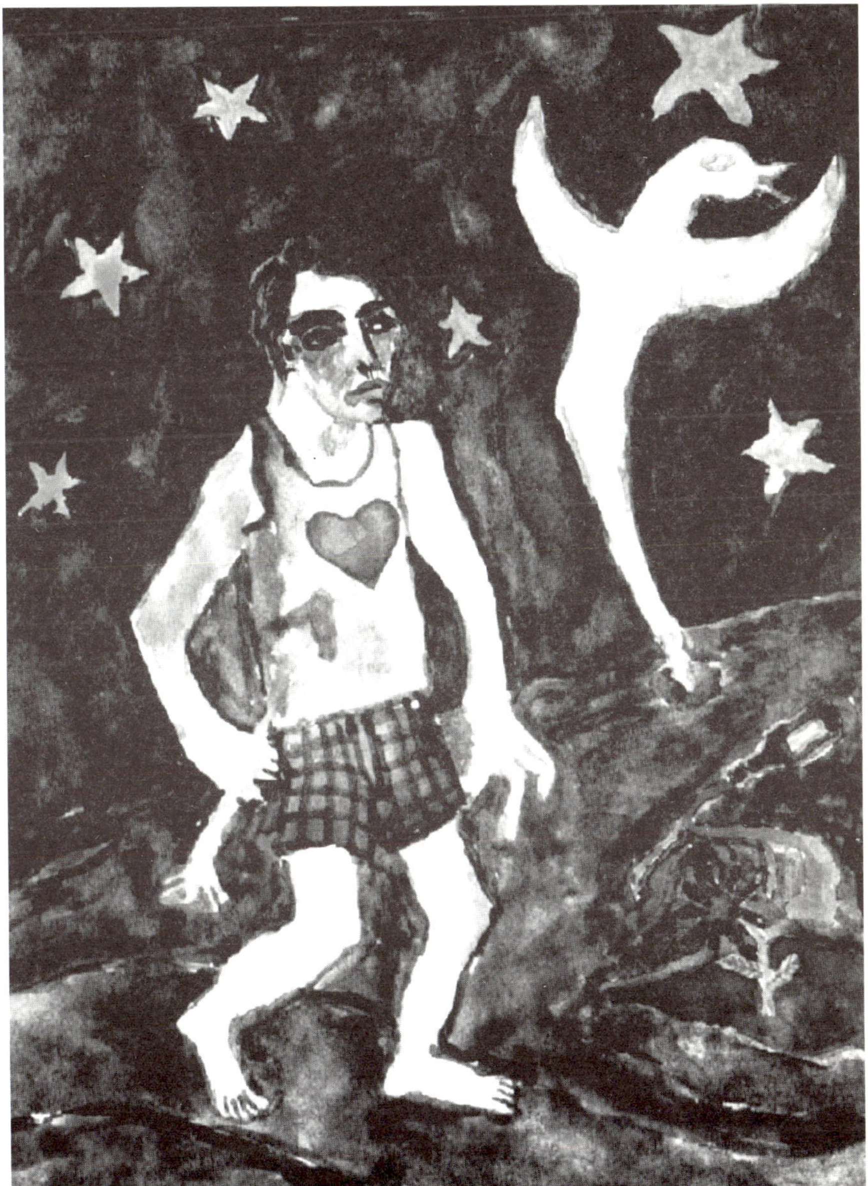

sean burn

Leeds, England

jackson pollock

    yr untitled
        yr destruction

           ov paintin
yr yellow island rituals ov mind
splashed out
eructin
yrs

 yr
    car horn route maps
in pink   blues   white
   ash   night

great arabesques
ov ink & air

ov carved bone
& the
   industrial
   minin
   the aluminium
   the phosphorescent
   the freeform
   sax sounds
   fog liftin
   over blue poles
   the wailin city

summertime's
somewhere
around dawn

sellin january

tryin sunglasses in the 2 way glass
in the t.k. maxx mirrors   sales now on
no buyin but howlin in leopard print
to the subliminals ov a bittersweet symphony
this isn't   but a cat callin cat walkin
a swirlin a struttin their almost
perfect size 12 stuff in fake fur &
crushed velvet boots & their laffin?

the brightest thing outov this day
since those earlier cheers in stereo
from out radio rentals

news
ov shearers 1st goal since 1998

134, #2

aa'm goin thru the old tenants mail
rippin open
their   private
their   confidential
their   private & confidential
important   do not ignore
we intend to disco...

what d'ya wanna be 11.9% call me c'mon call use sara's address
the benefits are   useful services are   yr references are

imperial locks
gift worlds
tempest funeral services
unisex hair stylists

@ the new harvest
the christ fellowship
get free
depression drugs pain sin quorn

tick if yu intend to contest jurisdiction
tick if yu intend to defend this claim

do be doo   be doo   be doo   do be doo be doo be doo be doo be doo

virgil suarez
Tallahassee, USA

Postal

There he stood, Charles Bukowski
behind the USPS counter, his hair
smoothed back, his beautiful
face like Montfort's lens
knew it: hard, tough.

He worked fast & steady,
his eyes friendly & focused,
the hands of a prince

    & when he called out "next"
    & I walked up to him, he smiled,
    & I greeted him.

His skin was not that bad, after all.
He knew why I needed
so many IRCs.

I ordered
a sheet of the new Fitzgerald
22 cent stamp.

He cut a glance at me.
"Not impressed," he said,
"not with the writing,
not with the man."

What about those green lights?
    I asked.

"Never mind
his green dock lights," he said,
"or mine. Write about your
own damn lights
& whatever you do
make them shine, shine
bright & long."

Las Palomas Voladoras, or How Cubans Came to Know Their Bicycles

In 1994 with the oil crisis in Cuba,
they imported Chinese bicycles
so that people could get to work,

go to school, exercise, and some
were welded-stretched into ten-seaters,
biciguaguas, people call them, bicycle-

busses, and the poor sap in front
pedalled the hardest while the man
in the back didn't, he just watched

or read the newspaper, so much like
communism, some said and feared
those words, and one day a child

looked out his window, set aflutter
a flock of pigeons perched on clothes-
lines, and he screamed "*palomas voladoras*"

and the name stuck, now when some
ride home, they flap their arms
in hopes that maybe they get there faster.

When the Great Chinese Papermakers Came to Cuba, the Great Poets Followed

because of the great stillness, a silence so deep it made the pink carp
rise to the pond's surface in hypnotic slumber, because an egret's crest

is blood red, a clenched fist, lips mouthing the air in Os, a tiger's
stealth among the bamboo forest, a hummingbird's delight in hibiscus,

dizzied by the flashes of sunlight echoed in its petals, because back home
the rain riveted the roofs of old lovers, a rumor of anguish, unreciprocated,

in Havana, one look at the harbors, beyond it toward Regla, the way boats
took on an air of oak leaves strewn on the horizon, an act of forgetfulness,

into the pulp goes their memories of a homeland, people, animals, scenes
of far-gone childhoods, a training of the spirit to hear everything;

they've come to speak silence into paper, the lost language of cranes,
a parrot's reputation for beauty, the way so many yearn for smooth, clean

surfaces, this heavenly paper upon which to write a first, lasting word.

Bay of Pigs Revisited

In 1966 my godmother/aunt Aleida came to visit Havana because she was getting married in Las Villas and she wanted my mother, the seamstress, to make her a dress from a special piece of cloth for which one of my mother's sister had traded two pigs and a goat. The piece of cloth was a parachute that had fallen out of the sky during the Bay of Pigs invasion. All that remained of the survivor was a fading hand print. My mother and aunt told stories as to what had been the fate of the parachuter as he plummeted from the sky on to a hostile beach. Surely, they contemplated, he died in the struggle and this was his hand pinked on to the material by the soldier's blood.

none of us knew the color of the ground
when we fell from the sky, hung
in the air, parachutes opening like Medusas,
while the sound of the planes faded

bullets pierced the skin, riddled the bodies
as we fell on to the sand, we fell dead, wounded,
in *camera lenta*, on to the sand, our blood
stained and dissolved in familiar waters

we stood and delivered until every magazine
emptied, cease fire called, we dropped our weapons
and surrendered, walked under palmeras
up the beach, hands up behind our heads,

boots sinking in the sand, while black birds flew
over the strewn corpses, and some, stuffed,
perched on the broken bodies, preened their feathers
others pecked tongues and plucked the eyes

of familiar faces, we, the survivors, moved
single file down the beach as we listened
to the silence that arose from the shore
to the silence that arose from the shores of exile.

Canticle of the Breasts

Lucky Teiresias who carried his own,
a hundred of them, the story goes,
given to him for peeping. At night,

you can fondle yourself to sleep.
Those of us who've consumed enough
chicken hormones develop our own

by the time we are 12. I'm talking
about boys, men, men like me who
stopped working out shortly after

thirty, and now the pectorals hang
there timid, pendulous, aware of no
returns to a previous hardness.

Soon I will be like one of those old
men at the park in their undershirts,
folds of skin on his lap, breasts

hung over the folds. But I promise
to wear mine proud, for it will have
taken as many years to carry them

so well, so far, when old men become
old women, and like death, well,
it's hard not to appreciate good breasts.

Distopia, or Bhaktin & Derrida Mud-Wrestle For Fun & Profit

Sure, it begins with insults, a hissed word about fragmentation
here, how words are merely symbols, road signs for the blind,

the big wrecking ball of deconstructionists, a brick-upon-brick
of desire, this language of moths driven to light because they

know not better. Pugilism is dead, who said? Watch these boys,
the one weighing one-hundred and seventy-five pound, with blue,

red and white shorts, France's colors? The one who speaks
with a lisp throws a mean jab, punches the color of grapefruit.

Think of any moment in your life, and you will fall backward
into a knot of blasphemy, memory's inner tube, what keeps all

of us from putting a bullet between the eyes. Who believes
Camus anymore? Sartre? Those nihilist princes of those dark,

dark moods, when even words can take flight against penumbra,
el escombro de las memorias, in Spanish, words as fists, punch-

drunk, let us all become a little nutty, soft around the waistline,
wear these thousand dollar shark-skin suits, Armani, Dior,

Yves St. Laurent, call the trainers, here comes the first blood,
straightened out the septum, rub Vaseline on all those cut brows,

remove the rubber teeth guards, let these boys speak, growl
about how language is more than pain, more than first blows.

felicity tumpkin
Zimbabwe, Africa

Underneath

He has found the combination to her mind
It is not a set of numbers.

A swell of letters shape
a pastiche of moments
on the patina of her brain

Hidden underneath
the thick skin
lies a yummy praline centre
He licks starving linear lips
slobbers, swallows his dribble

The cat mistakes the glow in his eyes
for the yellow of a streetlight
walks into it
dies.

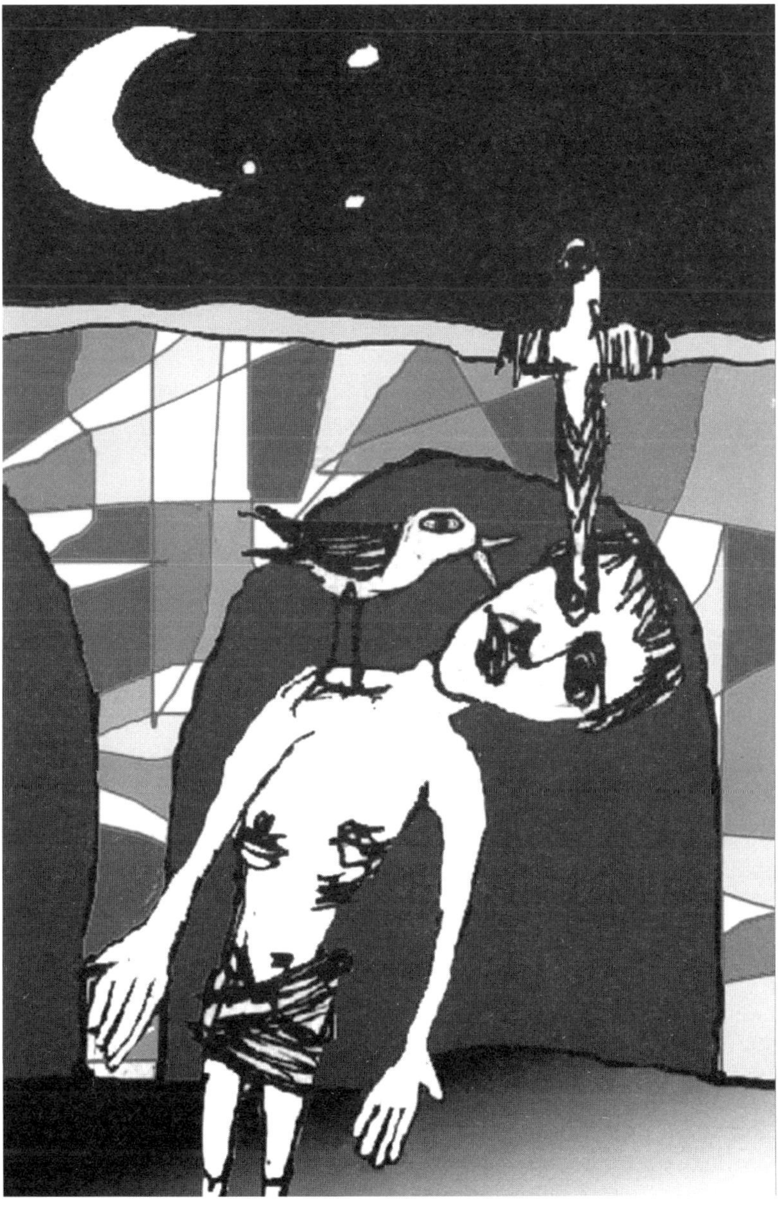

steve timms
Oldham, England

Compilation

"Think about me when you play. "
A C90 chrome dioxide cassette,
lovingly assembled and recorded
on a mid-price Sony CD-Radio:

the cover, a home made collage,
with comedian Jim Bowen's face,
gloriously highlighted in orange felt tip;
floating, eerily Oz-like, over
a metropolitan city sky-line.

Side A track I: The Lotus Eaters
with *"First Picture of You"*;
heard seeping through a grease
spattered radio in a Bradford cafe,
one sunny hung-over Sunday.

Track 3: your brother lurching through
Whigfield's *"Saturday Night "*, at
Julie's wedding; the finer points of the
intricate choreography, cruelly ousted
by a drunken Fred Flintstone stomp.

Side B, track 1: our first snog,
swallowed to Primal Scream's *"Loaded"*;
an inebriated kiss and knee trembler,
scored behind the kitchen bins
of a top Huddersfield night club.

Bonus holiday track: *'La Dolce Vita"*,
by Ryan Paris. You, dizzy with sun stroke,
collapsing outside a taverna in Corfu.
The former Euro-pop king briefly

glimpsed on a badly tuned television.
Track 7, side B: driving back
from a weekend in Scarborough:
Colourbox and *'The Moon Is Blue"*,
off a 4AD compilation tape,
free with the NME in 1988.

You switched it off, and after
the tears, we drove in silence.
No music, no sounds. Just the
soft thudding of windscreen wipers
and your strained, staccato breath.

"Think about me when you play",
read the smudged inlay inscription.
The tape ran out, the last song
a minute short. I don't know -

maybe you remember it differently.

steve sneyd
Huddersfield, England

Needing Ancestral Help

in preparation for a difficult meeting
reach across the centuries to where
generations long gone still suffer
inability to escape this sublunary sphere

if correctly you have named and summoned
inside you will upwell your forebear's succour
ring the bell as if quite ready for encounter
wait while footsteps pound down inside stair

just when the imphead doorknob turns and
the crack begins to widen but before you see
even eye of who holds your future tightest
twin fingers into throat and vomit

before the very polished feet the inward
ghost: then before you are spoken to or at, do
what you want most of all to do, avoid issue,
vanish into utterly cold-smelling fog

it brought you up you brought it up
all debts paid now and now you make
the great escape to where in turn you wait
to help the children you have made throw up

jacqueline karp
Vaux sur Mer, France

Yves

He went all of a sudden
without a fuss
not giving us time to say goodbye
carefully leaving the Greek homework marked
ready to give back
after the funeral.

Convenient being so alone -
just a few helpless friends regretting
they had not seen the signs or wondering
if they had really done enough.

His wide-eyed pupils, quiet –
fearful that death could brush against them so,
there in the classroom unannounced -
saw merely a slight failing
an arm grown stiff
face disobeying brain.

He walked away
neatly at the end of an exercise.
Declining help
he took his own bag
went with dignity
avoiding any bother.

Yves, you left us so suddenly
tiptoeing away
not taking the time to say goodbye,
but the Greek homework was marked
ready to hand back
after the funeral.

james prue
Brighton, England

Juggling On Brighton Beach

I taught Anil to Juggle
On Brighton Beach
First trip home
After Stuart died

If you drop a pebble
There's plenty more
So you can keep at it
'Til miraculously you find the rhythm
And the pebbles cycle round.
Something calming about that
You can't think about other things

But it doesn't last forever

At the funeral
Stuart's old school friend said
"Yes but could he really talk to you?"
Did we listen he means
A calm smiling face
Of accusation
And I couldn't say anything
Teeth clenched with
quiet anger

I'm just going for a walk he'd said
It was night time
A bit strange but Stuart was, at times.
And while we played cards into the night
He threw himself from
The top of the Richmond building.

andrew parker
Liverpool, England

Not Gospel

The brown-ness of your cunt skin
soft on my face
(Just it being there's a comfort)
Stomach InOut Breathing sounding
like your voice; a cloud.
Just know
it's only my opinion, it's not gospel
(or anything)

mary rudbeck stanko
Ontario, Canada

Zen Dream

All
of humanity
has been
given
a path to my
door.
Most delay
taking it,
but I
have been
the slowest of
All.

ken smith
Old Chatham, USA

Apples Be Damned

On the way to apple picking
with my two granddaughters,
Clouds of sheep in a meadow,
feral cats crown the roof of a derelict barn,
NO TURN ON RED ... STOP... YIELD...
TAKE ONLY TWO BAGS...NO SMOKING
NO EATING APPLES...NO CLIMBING...
I carefully recite the letters and words.
No teaching opportunity missed.
In an orchard of contorted trees
burdened with golden apples everywhere,
I award each a golden apple
and begin the story of Paris.
Both drop their apples.
The oldest, 4, seeks
only low climbing branches.
"UP, HANDS FIRST....DOWN, FEET FIRST,"
I drone and boost her up the tree.
She stretches for a higher branch with her foot.
The youngest, 2, seeks
only fistfuls of pebbles.
She drops them into a metal wagon.
She is her most appreciative audience.
She grins "apples be damned!"
I agree and fill my hands with stones.
My noise is louder and longer.
She removes my stones singly.
Exasperated, she exhales "you'll never learn."
She's right; I'm hopeless.

peter carpenter
Tonbridge, England

The Royal Scam

There you are in '76 on the Boulogne ferry,
hare-eyed from speed or dope, table covered
with empty bottles of export lager, a bulging nylon
rucksack, backrest and prop, patchworked
with badges from your Grand Tour. You spoke American
or Hollywood. Eyes shut, you leaned back in
apparent rapture, smoke rings managed from
each suck of *Marlboro*. Then we tried so hard
to stink of experience. We slugged *Stella*, swapped
fake tales of hitches, deals, that begging for pizza
on St. Germain. No contest. We'd reached
La Tranche Sur Mer. You'd just conquered
the known western world. You downed another
as the horizon dipped, rolled a joint with your toes.
Flaa-rence? (Port-holed profile now pure Giotto.)
Sur-real... We hid behind our last *Gitanes*
secretly yearning for clean sheets. For ages you rapped
above the swell, heir to every punchline until
you fell, grip gone on your carefully marked
Mythologies. Your final act, almost miraculous,
to hum exact a *Steely Dan* number in your sleep.
This is it, I thought, really it.
                              We took the air unsteady
out on deck. A sudden coolness. Unreal.

david roberts
Middlesbrough, England

Fisticuffs

He slapped me about
like a wet haddock.
Kicked me in the ribs,
karate chopped to the throat,
lamped me one in the eye.
Nutted me, kneed me,
kicked me in the nuts,
then pissed on me
even though I wasn't on fire.
A one sided competition;
I never could've been
a contender, small hands-
no spirit you see.

david lyall
London, England

April 1995, AD

In the British Museum
we walk among the ancient ruins.

5000 years of sun and windswept sand
have barely altered shape or rough contour
of layers of slow accumulated time.

We must avoid certain thoughts:
 we know our lives are small
but infinitely significant.

And what constitutes art
but smells and sights and desires?

Life, perfumed and imprisoned,
tell me I was right.

jacqueline sousa
Ryton, England

Door to Door

The same road which shocks you
with your first sight of a dead dog,
is flanked by woods so recessed
you imagine the seasons don't bother,
and a field where ponies graze belly deep
in wild flowers.
A power station takes over,
jostled by railway lines,
a white bath slumps near the track,
a pink dummy lolls in the gutter,
behind the hoardings wharves dress up
as developments.

jo pearson
York, England

Going to the Bottle Bank

Better move quick off that
best seat in the house
I'm going cheap, look,
there's plenty of me here
at one ninety nine
and 15 per cent proof.

Forget the leccy,
housework, that shave
you were going to have,
those January bills
and come and get
five bottles of me
any less would be an insult.

Don't be slow now
I'm running out fast
you'll find me somewhere
way at the back
that Lara Croft shimmy
you've perfected for hours

and take me there
to where I belong against your lips
your rough stubble
smelly tee shirt,
bare wet toes.

brendan mcmahon
Codnor, England

Evening

One evening she was
sad as a railway station

into infinite circles she
jacknifed like a bird

floated over mountains,
was mirrored like the sea

curled now like a sleeper
or another old song.

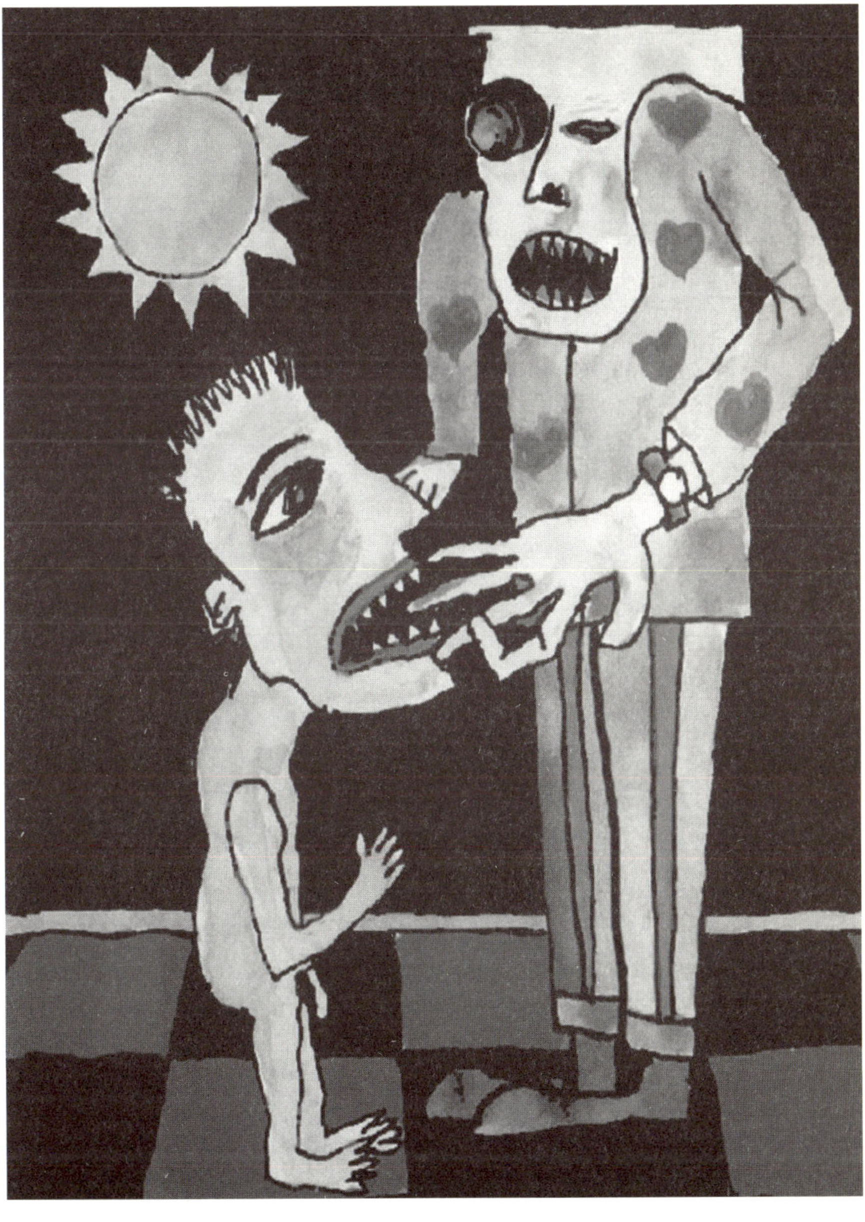

dave newman

Pittsburgh, USA

Gravity

I was at a truckstop somewhere in Iowa when a cop drove through the parking lot with his siren on. I was topping off my rig with 50 gallons of fuel. The squad car was a good hundred feet away but I flinched, thinking about the heroin I had stashed in my truck. It was only a couple bags, fifty bucks worth, but still. At this point, even traveling with a handful of pills made me nervous. Jail was on the bottom of my things-to-do list. So was losing this job. After I'd quit at the warehouse, my options were thin. It was running paper across the country or minimum wage at the mall.
I went inside, paid, came out, parked my rig. It was early afternoon. The sun was up. A cutting wind blew across the flat stretches of asphalt. The lot was almost empty, a dozen or so tractor trailers taking up the 100 plus spaces. I was bored, a little lonely, not desperate, but confident that there were better things to do than wait in Iowa with a load of paper that wouldn't deliver for three more days.
I turned on the radio. The big rock station played heavy metal, thrash, and a rap-rock hybrid. You think Iowa, you think farmers, corn, wheat. Break out the fiddles. Tune up the banjos. Kick up some dust at a hoe-down. The geography screamed acoustic guitar, mandolin, upright piano. The music I imagined was played on wood and string instruments that mostly needed strumming. The radio said different. The radio was obnoxiously loud and furious. Song after song demonstrated a love affair with electricity, a bad attitude, and the inability to actually sing. Each song was worse than the previous, all of it alien to the old white barns on the side of the road and the cows wandering the green fields.
The Midwest was weird like that.
The last time I'd passed through, I'd met a bunch of white kids who talked like they were from South Central LA. "Yo yo yo, G, whaz up, nigga?" It was a parallel universe of gangsta farmers. In Compton, were there black guys dressed in overalls who drove around on John Deere tractors and

listened to Hank Williams? "Y'all crackers coma back now, hear?"

I switched off the radio.

I checked my Timex. The second hand, tired of being watched, ran a sluggish race around its 60 second track.

The thought of more boredom, days of boredom, a weekend of cramped spaces and nothing to do, gave me an enormous headache. I'd developed a tolerance to aspirin so huge that anything less than a half dozen Bufferin was worthless so I massaged my temples and feigned prayer. On cue, the muscles in my lower back cramped, the annoyed fibers stretching out after sitting for hours on end, barely moving from slouch to straight. I rubbed my neck, I arched this way and that, I tried to clear my mind, but it was useless because the body required motion and the brain demanded stimuli. The head and heart were being cheated on a daily basis, and they were sick of it.

If you're a drug user, a drinker, whatever, all of which I was, this was the time for drugs, drinks, whatever, or, since I was holding, heroin.

Truck driving was an awful job. This was my second try. The first attempt ended almost as soon as it started. I was home for a weekend after 45 days on the road and went out with my friend Franny. We started late, bar hopped until two.

After The Tavern closed, we hit a party. I drank some, not too much, maybe a dozen or so beers all night. Later, around five in the morning, on our way home, a cop flashed his lights and I slowed down, hoping he'd pass on the left. He didn't so I pulled onto the berm and hit the hazards. Franny had a can of Rolling Rock beer between his legs that I hadn't noticed before. I turned on the dome light. In the glovebox, I found my registration. My license was in my wallet. The cop knocked on the driver's side window. Rap, rap. Flashlight beams flooded the car. I knew. Franny knew. The cops knew. It was over in seconds.

The cop said, "Okay, I'm gonna have to ask you to put your hands behind your back," in a firm but gentle fashion that gave little indication that he was wrecking my life.

I said, "Are those bracelets really necessary?"
He said, "You bet they are."
I watched my head as I climbed in the squad car. The cuffs cut my wrists. I was numb with depression. By then, the other cops had Franny in cuffs, too. They drove him home in another black and white, talking tough, threatening to charge him with an open container violation. It was a sad, pathetic night. Sitting in the back of the squad car as we rode off towards the hospital and the blood test, I chatted up the officers and hoped they'd come around and cut me some slack, but they didn't. They ushered me into the ER where a nurse jabbed at my arm in hopes of finding a vein. Ten minutes later, outside, in the parking lot, as the rain drizzled down, they slapped the cuffs back on and started talking about a night in county jail or whether I could be released on my own recognizance. While waiting on their verdict, I fumbled with the abstract math of alcohol, body weight, and transportation, giving five to one odds that I was over the legal limit. The legal limit was a joke. What I'd do for money or where I'd work„ I honestly didn't know.
The whole process took a year but I finally lost my license which cost me the job. Fortunately, I lucked into the gig at the warehouse. The work wasn't much but it paid. I started loading boxes, worked my way up to supervisor. I began thinking the DUI was a blessing in disguise. Supervision was easier than driving an 18 wheeler. Paperwork beat living in a bunk. Then I hit a guy in the face with a clipboard and broke his nose. It was a complex story, one that involved a kind, gentle midget, some goons, and the attempt to take away a co-worker's dignity. Eventually, under pressing circumstances, I quit. Even though I hated trucking with a passion, I still believed I'd done the right thing. You can't just beat a midget to hell and back for being short and squatty.
Back in my truck in Iowa, I put my face flat against the steering wheel and honked the city horn with my forehead. Honk, honk. I did it again and again.

At truckstops, hookers come knocking on your door in the wee

wee hours, offering 10 dollar handjobs, 20 dollar blowjobs, and 30 dollar fucks. Almost always, the women are fat, unpleasant, and butt-ugly. They reek of wine and smoke. They dress in jeans and flannels like men. They steal. They are perpetually black and blue. They complain about bad tricks. They seldom get work. The work they get is low. Once, a woman with a gob of undetected jizz in her hair, offered to blow me for cigarettes and a six pack of Schlitz. I gave her ten bucks and some silver change to go away.
Ultimately, you're better off at a whorehouse.
Three months prior, on my last visit to Corn Heaven, someone pounded on my truck window around midnight. In a deep sleep, I imagined a beautiful whore with all her teeth.
Hanging by my driver's side door were six young farmboy-gangstas, white kids, making a sales pitch on an ounce of weed. They dressed in baggy jeans that didn't fit, black knit caps, huge puffy coats. Under the moon, they shucked and jived, rapping violently about the excellence of their pot.
"Yo yo yo, G, dis shit is from South America."
"Muthafuckin weed make you fly."
"Dis shit is da chronic, my man, I ain't rollin ya here."
I said, "South America? Come on, you're selling South Iowa dirt weed. Who are you kidding?"
"Naw."
"Naw, G."
"Naw, naw, we ain't playin ya. Dis shit da chronic."
I messed with my hair. That morning, after four scuzzy days, I'd showered in Wisconsin and still felt clean.
The smallest one, a five foot hoodlum who looked 15 and wore his Oakland Raiders knit hat pulled so low I could barely see his eyes, climbed on the running boards of my truck to bargain down and cut me a deal. I leaned out the window, elbow first. I sensed they didn't have guns or were too nice to use them. The exteriors were tough. Underneath, they were pups.
I said, "What's up, dopeman?"
He said, "For you, my man, half off. We wanna ditch that chronic then roll. We got bitches to skin."
"Yeah, G, bitches to skin. We runnin muthafuckin late."

"Rollin, rollin, rollin, keep them bitches rolling, rawhide!'" one of them sang.

Oh god, the comedy. I was ready to burst. Dopeman handed me the bag for inspection. The pot was the green of fresh cut grass. I shook it down.

I said, "Look, I couldn't buy it if I wanted to. I get drug tested and pot stays in my system too long."

Dopeman took the bag. "You sure, G? Last chance."

I said, "What else you got?"

He said, "Aw ight, now ya kickin it, aw ight."

I was always looking for pills. The hours required to truck were impossible without medication.

Dopeman handed over a bag filled with capsules. I looked them over, smelled the bag, took out a couple.

I said, "I don't want these."

"G, them's ups. They keep you sky all night. You know dat, m'brutha."

I said, "Dopeman, they're fucking Tylanol."

Dopeman said, "How you know that, money?"

I said, "They say Tylenol right on the fucking capsules. You need to do your homework."

Dopeman said, "Good goddamn, what the fuck."

I said, "No kidding, good goddamn."

This was taking the crushed up aspirin bit to new lows. The next step up was selling oregano as marijuana, pissed on paper as LSD. What a pathetic con.

Dopeman hopped down and circled his posse. They all stood rigid with fear or, maybe, embarrassment. One lonely G botched his chance to make good. After another interrogating lap and a few fake punches, Dopeman kicked the shortest fattest boy in the lag. Dopeman laid down some boot. Step, kick. Step, kick. Plant. Ha worked his knee. The fat kid jump-stepped away.

Dopeman said, "Ya fucked up again, dawg."

Fat Dawg said, "Quit ya fuckin kickin me. I ain't ya fuckin bitch. Quit bangin me, dawg."

After another fake punch, they settled down, even Dopeman, each one scratching their boots against the pavement, stuffing their hands in the front pockets of their jeans which drooped down below their waists.

To make a joke, I said, "Where'd you guys get those funny accents."

Dopeman said, "Shit, we lived in Iowa our whole muthafuckin lives," as if that explained it all, as if white people calling each other niggas was indigenous to the Midwest.

I shook my head, laughed. Their collective confusion was mind-blowing. It cleared out the cobwebs. With the cool air blowing on my face, I knew I'd never get back to sleep, not that it mattered. The load I was sitting on didn't deliver until noon. I was ready to buy something.

I said, "Where's a good nudie bar?"

Dopeman said, "Aw, the good ones are closed or closing soon enough." Then, to his homies, "Go try to peddle that shit, dawgs. I got ta tells you everyfuckinthing?"

The boys dispersed.

I said, "Well, where's a crummy nudie bar that's open?"

He said, "The Green Bean's down the road."

"The what?"

"The Green Bean. I told ya, man, this is fuckin Iowa. I-owa. I-0-fuckin-wa. Everything here is fucked the fuck up."

The Green Bean was an old whorehouse busted down to a sorry-ass strip club that looked like a double wide trailer. There were three strippers, all plump, a bouncer, also plump, and an oldies jukebox that was thin on tunes. The bathrooms reeked. The wood bar was carved up with names and initials. The disco ball hung from the ceiling like a deflating balloon. The overhead lights were all purple and didn't flash.

The bartender was a 300 pound women with a bleached blonde mustache and a Dutch Boy hairdo. She was built like a bowling ball on stilts. She had no waist, no tits, no real ass to speak of, essentially unisexual, and I would have mistaken her for a man if she hadn't introduced herself as Sally while extending a fat hand with long elegantly painted fingernails.

I said, "Sally, let me have 20 singles, a shot of something sweet, and a Coors in a bottle."

She said, "We have Coors Light in cans."

I said, "That'll do."
Two old truckers sat at the far end of the bar. Other than that, the place was empty. I took my stack of singles to the railing by the stage.
A stripper said, "Holy shit, a paying customer." With both hands, she stretched out the white tanktop she was wearing like it might actually quit clinging to her tits. She adjusted each breast, bent at the waist, and shook out her hair. She stood up, turned around, and, with one finger, dug her red bikini from the crack of her ass.
I said, "Nice outfit."
The other two strippers fluffed up. The short redhead wore a tacky, babyblue feather boa. The tall brunette sported a black silk bathrobe with some red oriental writing which she quickly shed to reveal a purple g-string, a purple and black push-up bra, and two huge fake boobs like tires holding 30 pounds of air.
Twenty bucks wasn't going to last very long.
The one said again, "Holy shit, are you really here to spend money?"
I said, "I guess so."
Suddenly, I wasn't so sure. I took a long guzzle of beer. It tasted like warm tin and peroxide.
Feather boa said, "I get next dance, no question about it. I'm not even joking around here."
Fake boobies said, "I'm next, bitch, check the schedule."
They moved off to the side, chatting up the bouncer who was trying to regain consciousness. He looked my way, lifted his big tattooed arm, and waved like a tired girl before leaning back against the plywood wall in a slump. He was high on something. Pills, dope, opium, whatever, lots of it. I knew it, and was jealous. To be that far gone and still on your feet was looking like the way to go.
The remaining stripper extended her hand to shake. In her other hand she held a box camera, one of those throw-away deals.
She said, "Hi, I'm Marissa, and I guess I'll be your stripper for the night."

I said, "Hi, I'm Dan," and couldn't think of anything witty to add as we shook hands. "What's with the camera?"
"This?" she said, snapping my picture from the hip.
I said, "Well, there goes my career in politics."
She said, "Do you even want me to dance? This is about stupid, isn't it?"
I said, "I have 20 bucks here."
I held up the money. She snapped another picture, this time of my hand clutching the bills.
Within an hour, the other dancers, best girlfriends, serious partners, would call it an early night. Without much thought, I'd lean into Marissa and kiss her on the mouth. The bouncer would be face down on the bar by then, Sally in the back counting money, and the old truckers dried up and long gone. Marissa would say, "Not here, I'll get fired."
Later, after we'd fucked all night, she'd blow me in the basement of her grandmother's house.
I conked out in my bunk and woke up at five. With the engine off, the truck was freezing. I stretched out under the covers. It was depressing living in such small quarters, what basically amounted to a twin bed. On my mattress, I read, ate, and drank, propped up to various degrees with pillows. With luck, I sometimes fucked here, rocking the whole cab with strange women I'd never see again. Even under the best of circumstances, the lack of space was trying. Every morning, I dressed flat on my back, struggling with my clothes.
Afternoon had given over to twilight. The parking lot was packed. I scooted behind the steering wheel to get comfortable. After turning the key, I hit the starter. The cold diesel engine turned over with a chug.
Out of habit, I flipped on the radio, hitting seek. Guitar, drums, vocals, guitar solo, dopey lyrics, same old shit. The once noble roots of radio were long gone, variety lost to programming, personality to dullness, voice and talent to the drum machine. Radio's lone virtue was that it announced the weather with some regularity. Outside of the forecast, it was sad DJs, jerkoff politics, and toilet humor. If I wanted tunes,

I swerved down the Interstate, fumbling with the tape player, ejecting Hank Williams for Billie Holiday, Billie Holiday for Townes Uan Zandt, Townes for Ray Charles who sang old-time country with more soul than any frequency allowed.
From under my seat, I grabbed my address book. Marissa's phone number was somewhere in there but I couldn't find it. At the payphone outside the restaurant, I dialed information. The operator picked up.
I said, "How many numbers can I get? Three? Okay, I need one for The Green Bean. Yes, it's a business. Actually, no, it's a strip club. Okay, and the other one is for JC Penny's. No, it's not a strip club, it's the department store. Yeah, I got the joke, very funny. No, that's it, those two are all I need. Thank you very much."
The receiver was an icecube against my ear. I hung it up and thought about what to do.
Marissa stripped nights, worked days at a mall photography studio. She fingered herself for tips. She snapped happy family portraits. I couldn't imagine the contrast. Nude dancing, kiddie photos. The lengths we go to to make a living are impossible to comprehend.
She'd said, "I strip for money, sure. But I love, love love absolutely love, taking pictures."
I'd said, "Ever mix things up?"
"What? Like wear my g-string to JC Penny's? Duh."
With a little confusion or a deliberate blending of the two professions, she could've been a huge star in the porno industry. I said as much, jokingly, but she didn't blink when she admitted the idea had crossed her mind.
I dialed JC Penny's and asked for Marissa.
A youngish sounding girl who identified herself as Janice after offering me a limited deal on a free eight by ten, said, "God, yeah, we're her answering service here," in a disgusted voice then put me on hold, clicking the line over to lite rock for my listening pleasure.
A couple minutes later, Marissa said, "Hello."
I said, "Hey, this is Dan Charles," and immediately felt stupid for using my full name.

"Dan Charles, holy shit. You know what? Believe it or not, I just developed some pictures of you like two days ago. Holy shit, this is really unbelievable. I didn't think I'd ever hear from you again."
It was almost impossible to be a trucker and not ooze desperation. I was wondering if I'd made a mistake by calling. I said, "I'm in Iowa."
"You're kidding? Really, god, come see me."
"Now?" I said, feeling more relieved.
"Yeah, now. I have a 30 minute break coming up."
"Ah, I'm scuzzy. Why don't you meet me somewhere after you work. Better yet, come pick me up at the truckstop. I'll buy you something to eat."
"I have to work," she said, her voice going to a scratchy whisper, "at the club. But you can come see me there. We hired more dancers. I'll have lots of time to talk."
"What time?"
"Ninish, something like that. I'm done here at eight, but I have to swing by the house and check on Grams."
Her grandmother, Grams as she sing-songally called her, had debilitating arthritis in her hands so she couldn't cook or clean very well anymore. Marissa lived in the basement and did most of the chores.
I said, "How late do you work?"
"Until close, but maybe I can sneak out. Business is picking up again but we're still not packed. If they let someone leave early, I'll make sure it's me."
"Okay, I'll drink in my truck for a while and come over around ten or so. Sound good?"
"No, god, don't drink in your truck, that's nasty. Go to the club and drink with Sally. She'll remember you."
I said, "Fat Sally?"
She said, "Yes, Fat Sally, but that's not very nice." Then, "Where are you staying?"
"The penthouse at The Sands. Come on, where do you think?"
"Don't stay in that dirty truck. You can come stay with me. Do you want to stay with me?"
I said, "Yeah, I want to stay with you." Then, toning it down,

"I mean, is it okay if I stay with you?"
"God, yes, this is a stupid conversation. Let's just say whan you're in Iowa, you stay with me-- how's that? You can stay right up until I say you can't stay anymore."
"Okay, I'll cancel my reservation at The Sands."
"Hold on for one second. My boss is calling me."
An old JB Hunt cabover rolled by and dropped the windchill another 20 degrees. Without the sun, it was freezing. I jumped in place to keep warm. I lifted my knees, jogged a two-step circle. I was excited. At rare moments, trucking lifted the ugly black cloud of work to reveal the blue sky of adventure. I thought about how much fun I'd had with Marissa during our last night.

At one point, during our first night together, after The Green Bean closed and Marissa swerved backroads home, after small talk, and after sex, she said, "Let me take one of you naked."
"A picture?" I'd said.
"Duh, of course, a picture."
"No way."
"Great, let me get my camera. This will be fantastic. Stay right there."
"Pay attention. I said, Nuh huh, no way."
I grabbed her as she flopped her legs over the edge of the waterbed. The sheets were pink silk, tacky, straight out of a cartoon whorehouse, and she slid back on a small tidal wave. We were at an awkward angle so her tits came down across my face, the top of her head knocking into the headboard. Things went, respectively, splosh and thud.
Rubbing her head, she said, "That smarts."
I said, "No kidding," and grabbed at one of her tits with my mouth in a loud sucking motion.
She said, "Kiss gentle. They get really sore right before my period."
She sat up, straddling my chest, her heavy thighs pressing into my ribs. Inches from my face was her nicely manicured pussy. Minutes before, this would have been intensely sexual,

something to penetrate with my fingers, my cock, or my tongue, but now, post-orgasm, her shaved bush and pink lips were nice, bordering on lovely, feminine but without much draw. I don't know how it is with other men, but after sex, I am without it: sex, the drive, everything. I am clear thinking and laid back.

She said, "Come on, come on, let me take a photo of you, as is, all sweaty and everything." She gave me a squeeze with her legs. "Look, I'll frame you with my knees. After that, we'll shoot our way down." She did some fake pictures, snapping her finger over an imaginary camera, making her mouth pop like a flash bulb.

I said, "Out of the question," not mentioning that the time to ask was during sex when I was vulnerable and up for anything.

She said, "Why?"

I said, "Why?" like that was even a question.

"Yeah, why?"

"Why? I'm fucking fat for one. I've gained 20 pounds since I started trucking. Furthermore, I have a small dick."

In a gymnastic move, she arched back and cupped my balls, pumping them a few times like a squeeze toy she expected to squeak, gradually switching to a rattling motion, side to side, as if my testicles might clack and make sounds. She finished the maneuver with a firm shake of my prick like it was an extended hand at an important business meeting. It was a funny gesture, not meant to be sexual, but it was. Some blood flushed down there and I realized I was going to be ready sooner than expected.

She said, "I think you have a nice package. Why are men so obsessed with size? Size isn't everything."

"I'm not obsessed with penis size."

"I think it's a nice package."

"It's a great package. I just don't think it's all that photogenic." Jokingly, I added, "But you can photograph my balls all night long."

Jokingly, she said, "Balls aren't artistic. They come in that wrinkled-up bag." Then, "Do you think I'm fat?" She patted

her stomach which was firm but not without some pudge.
I said, "Not at all. Why? Do you think you're fat?"
"No, I think I'm great. Some guy said I was fat the other night. I think I'm built like Betty Page. Voluptuous."
"I like that word. Voluptuous."
She said it again. Voluptuous. All those vowels. We sang it together, my hand reaching for her breast.
She scootched down my body. I kissed her mouth, once to be tender, again because it felt good. She put her lips to my neck and sucked at my ear. We rolled around, having fun, talking and kissing.
Marissa had big tits, a big ass, some belly, most of it solid, all of it curvy. When she was on top, I could feel it, gravity, the weight of her. With bleached-out blond hair, black roots, and too much powder caked on her rough skin, she appeared older than her years which I guessed to be 25. In most ways, she looked like you'd imagine a stripper to look like who worked at The Green Bean near the Super America truckstop in Iowa. I liked her face, its testimony to experience, but she wasn't pretty. She was, up close and at a glance, more sexual than anything else. She was comfortable with the way her body felt and moved. When she fucked, she didn't hold back. We ended up on our sides, my front to her back. I was three-quarters hard and started to wiggle inside her.
She said, "I'm a little sore," and turned back around to kiss my neck and ear. "But we can do this."
She rolled across me, darting downward. She propped up with an elbow, quickly got comfortable, and took my cock in her mouth. She took me inside and held me there. Literally, she sucked. The movements she used came just from inside her mouth, not her hand or neck. It lasted for only a few seconds, this sucking. After that, she went through various moves, licking a lot, each trick better than the next, until she found a slow steady pace where I went from her lips to her throat and back.
I couldn't see anything but her hair and the bobbing of her head so I turned my attention to her ass, her back, her waist, the way things fused together in a curve that sent more blood

to my cock. I put my hand on Marissa's hip and squeezed.
I said, in a quiet voice, "Do you want to 69?"
She didn't turn around but said, "Nuh huh, I'll just do you," then went back down with her mouth.
I put my hands behind my head so my arms formed wings, and got comfortable. I opened my eyes and looked around. I removed myself from the sex, temporarily. It was a whole apartment down there in Gram's basement. Kitchen, livingroom, bedroom, all divided up by cheap oriental screens or blankets that dangled from overhead pipes. In one corner, an old shower, dressed up with a black plastic curtain where pink butterflies flapped their wings. In another corner, a partially remodeled bathroom, awaiting a door and, from what I could see, a sink with some pipes.
I closed my eyes and thought of how great it would feel to come again after not doing any work.
Back on the phone, Marissa said, "Hey, I'm back. My boss is about a dickhead. I'm not supposed to get calls here."
I said, "Quit."
She said, "I can't. I need the money. And I use all their supplies for my pictures."
I said, "Call off at the other place. Can you do that?"
She said, "I don't know." Then, "Maybe, probably, I think so. I've never called off before. Call me back in half an hour."
I said I would.
Back in my truck, I dug through my duffel bag, looking for decent clothes, a towel to take inside the truckstop to use in one of their rundown showers.
Without meaning to, I came up with the heroin, one bag, a blue rubberband tight around the plastic.
Drugs are like that sometimes.
You're in the desert, eating sand, when the sky inverts with the ocean, and for an instant, before the gravity returns, you're walking on clouds, ready for rain, in awe of this miraculous gift of water which, in seconds, will return to the barren earth.
At which point, God gets pissed off and sends a great flood.

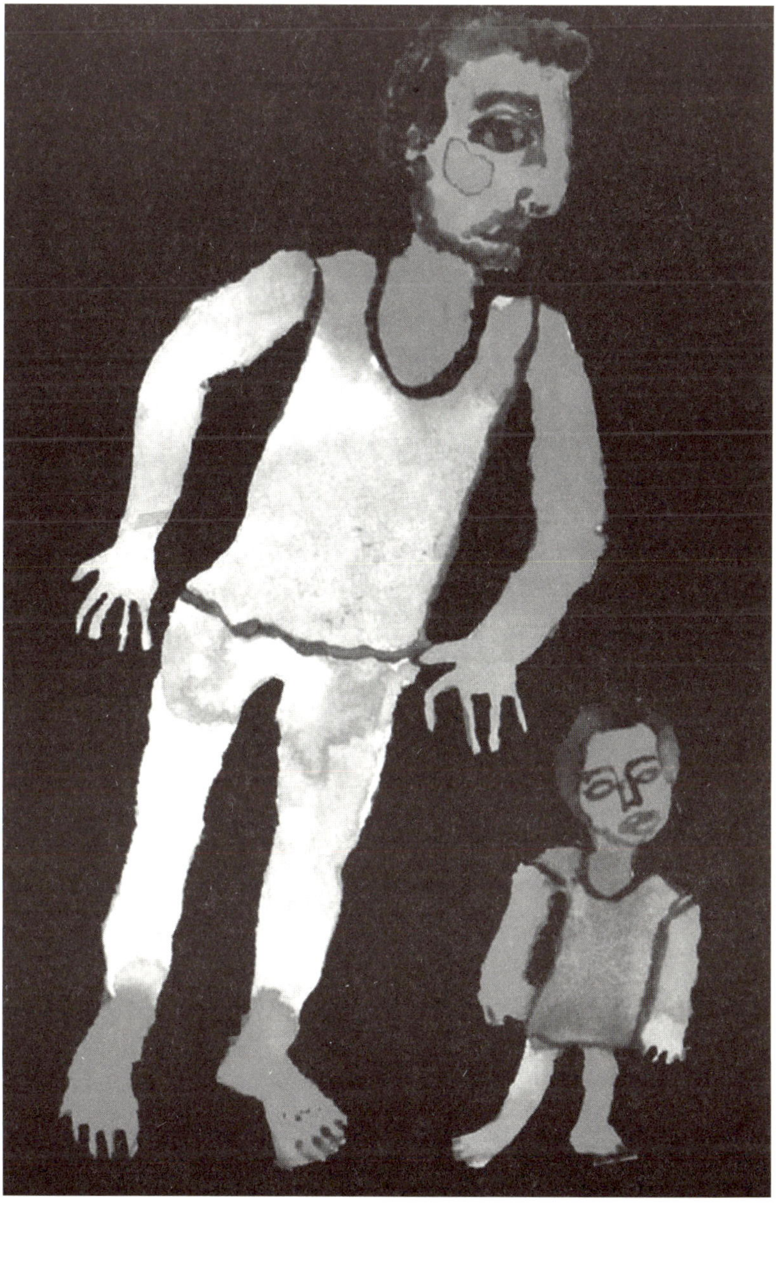

anna woodford
Newcastle, England

99% Perspiration

Studying the handbook not the exhibits,
pausing without thought, watching paint dried,
only Picasso to join the dots and I've got the Prado picture.
Ready for bullet-proof glass when the hooves run at me,
through my eye before my mind.
All down the wall the horse battles with perfection,
with the spear in its side,
the paint-stones hurled at its body.

In Vienna, gold frames wink like playboys,
send me off with the red-haired women to the top of the canvas.
Klimt lets his muses let their hair down like scarlet Rapunzels.

Genius is in the attempt.
I smuggle it out on postcards but it
won't be cut to size.

Evening Class

Every Monday I go to photography,
to open my apertures, have a stab in the dark room,
experiment with chemicals.
Next door they're on their second glass of wine,
across the corridor the mood is light as meringue –
while at home kids see to themselves.

At break we fill the partition crack
to become wallflowers at a line-dancing class.
Some people pick up their not-so-hot chocolate
quilted in fencing gear.

Every Monday I go to photography
to train my eye, frame my subject,
learn to see in black and white.
One wrongly-loaded film wrong-footed me from the start,
up and down the garden path firing blanks all week.

Every Thursday you learn Spanish,
language of the girl you left me for,
New phrases collect on your smooth tongue,
Your mouth runs to catch your wandering eye
like a hero in a baseball game. Good catch.

In the way you scavenge
when things fall apart,
for information – I know

your first date, when she stayed,
by heart.
Unlearning what I thought I knew.

Every week we expand separate horizons.

On Monday turning my negatives into a positive,
on Thursday you do the same.

finella davenport
Manchester, England

Skinheads, 1978

His face, black like olives
"Do you want to dance?"
I could feel myself sweating
He was too
My skirt was wet; if I moved
from the wall he'd think I'd pissed myself
"Do you want to dance?"

If only we weren't in
the bloody church hall
With all the young baldies'
Pale blue eyes staring over
tawny pints and stale
beef sarnies.

"Do you want to dance?"
He was tall, taller than me, taller
than anyone there
Harvest Sunday
The petals of flowers around my neck
falling like peeled skin
The scent of them stronger than opinion.
Yes, I want to dance.

On Skates

Uck. Uck. Uck.
4.6 4.5 4.9 4.2
Glide, as if you don't have legs.
Slide.
The rink is harder than the competition.
Glide, and remember team spirit.
5.2 6.0 5.2 4.9
They are judging everything
Every detail, every lift, every scrape in the frost
6.0 6.0 6.0 6.0
Glide, to be a winner
And to wear black skates with a very sharp blade
This is what it is to be a champion
In a cold sport.
Uck. Uck. Uck.

b. z. niditch
Brookline, MA, USA

Outside A Paris Cafe

Why do you think
the future is pink
and not a blue beret

it was that
chameleon smile
that intrigued the judge

where life is not respectable
and the true source
of the collapsible system

memory under grey memoir
and white nights
which hide the urchins

yet the judge
let you go
only for your own good

beyond the murder
of your only French roll
somewhere near the metro.

Old City

you walked
in the old city
with the aroma
of a green sea
within the fangs of silence
afraid to die in the next breath
of the caterpillar
a black car drives
on the deserted beach
a flailing lightning
unravels
near a boat
someone is bloodied up
looking for sea shells
and the boy
who was declared missing
starved on white rice
finds three coins
among the swine of occupation.

Imprimatur

He gave you his signature
hidden in blood and piss
but it was of no use
he wanted what he wanted
a man of thunder, Mars and S&M
who took you on his cycle
speeding off headlong
to your last stop.

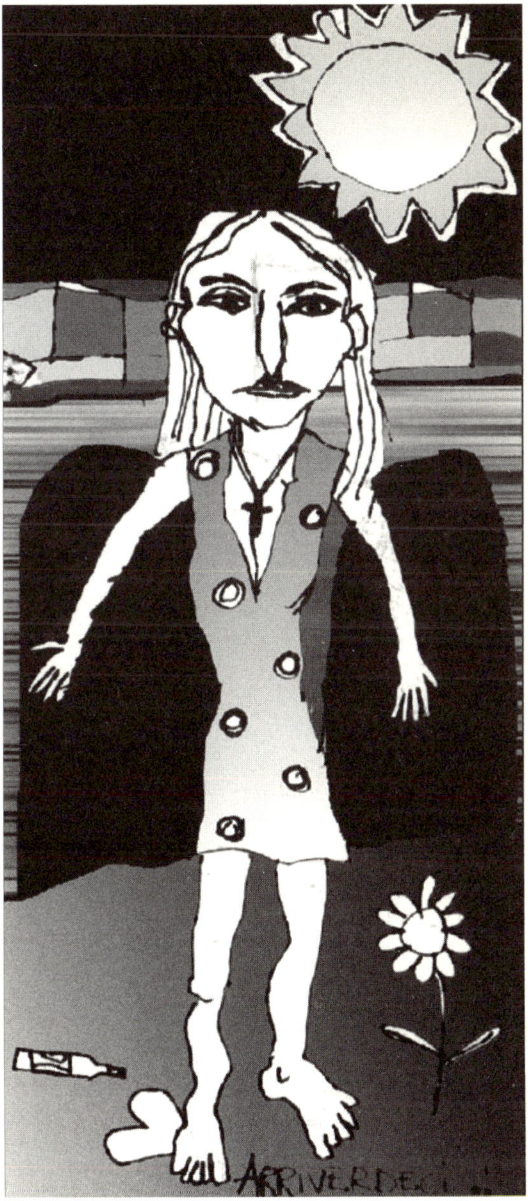
ARRIVERDECI

robert nazarene
Chesterfield, USA

Nutshell

I drink alone.
My wife's a cunt.

Kids? Yeah.
I got one.

He's got everything a boy could need:
mini-bike, Game Boy & gun.

At *The Pistol-Whip* Bar & Grill

It's dark inside *The Pistol-Whip*,
red neon spits: "We Never Close".
Longnecks a-buck-&-a-quarter...
& tall tales sprout from the rows

of wobbly stools, battered and torn,
with patches of masking tape,
where men with stout bellies bellow & bleat,
deciding on who get's the blame.

It's dark inside *The Pistol-Whip*,
but real men aren't shy with their views:
"If it wasn't for the niggers, the cunts and the kikes..."
(The lunchboxes *roar.!* their approval.)

"If it wasn't for this & for that & for this..."
(The piss funnels, warm, down the drain...)
"If only she'da gave me a second chance...
I'da blown that bitch into next week!"

Treebonics

- *Sign: Prairie Lights Bookstore / Cafe*
  Iowa City, Iowa

"Please take
napkins if
you need them,
but keep in mind
the trees..."

Dear Mistuh President:

    Y'all bins ta Georgetown.
Home, I bins ta Georgetown, 2!

    (Yo! lissen up, muthafucka!)

    Dey's a whole lotta shit
goin' down in de forust, dem
deers an' dem birds gettin' screwed.

    I knows I dont be's me
no scholar. Ya'll probly sats
closer in class.

    But a walk thru de woods
jus' ain't chillin' no mo', *Git dat*
lumberjack dick out yo' ass!

Little Mister

(after Maria McLeod)

Little mister big boss, Little mister
sport fan, Little mister back-slap,
Little mister shit grin, Little mister
big talk, Little mister gun show,
Little mister gold card, Little mister
Dow Jones, Little mister fake smile,
Little mister glad hand, Little mister
working late, Little mister can't cum,
Little mister cuss-a-lot, Little mister
gotta go, Little mister road rage, Little
mister peep show, Little mister
shiny shoes, Little mister new suit,
Little mister pickle park gruntin'
like a pig snoot, Little mister fat
mouth, Little mister answer man,
Little mister head nods, Little mister
Blam! Blam!

rosemary palmeira

Beverley, England

The Return

Forty, fifty years pass by
they are returning, one by one
defiant, broken, shaking.

Bitter and forgiving
tanned and scarred
wise-cracking and abject.

Hoping against hope.

It was the hardest thing he ever did
To walk, leaning upon another
The hall opening up the ocean
His legs almost giving way

To meet *Her.*

Crossing The Water

I stand at the shoreline between island and continent
So easy, so hazardous, to cross this water
I cross from my adult world back to childhood
Back to the walled house, the animals, the laughter.

I cross from my knowledge to my instincts
From air to earth, within the safe garden wall
And beyond that, the knife-grass and bittersweet stalks
And the sea, always the sea and the sea-glass fall.

Souls have drowned there, before I could know them:
My vivacious grandmother and her three young daughters
And eight cousins, mother and children. Who were they?
The waves have claimed them, the treacherous waters.

Dreams run over the edge, trailing colours and hopes
Children astride trees, climb almost to their prime.
Nothing left now but bones, washed bare of flesh
And grief, which does not heal, nor ease anytime.

Curled sepia photographs, newspaper cuttings
Memories are passed down, from a long time before
Oporto. 1942. Salazar leans to Mussolini.
A convoy of civilian ships go home, in time of war.

The *'Avocet'* sets sail, her upcurving beak
a prow, moving with the wind's chime
From underneath, a torpedo bursts inside her belly
Mortally wounded, she capsizes, lost for all of time.

I see them underwater, I see them in my sleep:
The ghost-woman, ghost-children, the family idyll
Their lovely names float like flowers, like jewels
Rosalie, Primrose, Hazel and Beryl.

A boy, stands and waits - his ship has docked;
But the *Avocet* is missing, to return no more.
He will never go back to the house of his childhood
He upturns his face to the hills, to the heart's core.

To my father Derek and his family: Rosalie, Primrose, Hazel and Beryl Cassels